HOUGHTON MIFFLIN LITERARY READERS

BOOK 2

HOUGHTON MIFFLIN COMPANY   BOSTON

Atlanta   Dallas   Geneva, Illinois   Palo Alto   Princeton   Toronto

Program Authors

William K. Durr, John J. Pikulski, Rita M. Bean, J. David Cooper, Nicholas A. Glaser, M. Jean Greenlaw, Hugh Schoephoerster, Mary Lou Alsin, Kathryn Au, Rosalinda B. Barrera, Joseph E. Brzeinski, Ruth P. Bunyan, Jacqueline C. Comas, Frank X. Estrada, Robert L. Hillerich, Timothy G. Johnson, Pamela A. Mason, Joseph S. Renzulli

Senior Consultants

Jacqueline L. Chaparro, Alan N. Crawford, Alfredo Schifini, Sheila Valencia

Program Reviewers

Donna Bessant, Mara Bommarito, Yetive Bradley, Patricia M. Callan, Clara J. Hanline, Fannie Humphery, Barbara H. Jeffus, Beverly Jimenez, Sue Cramton Johnson, Michael P. Klentschy, Petra Montante, Nancy Rhodes, Julie Ryan, Lily Sarmiento, Ellis Vance, Judy Williams, Leslie M. Woldt, Janet Gong Yin

Acknowledgments

For each of the selections listed below, grateful acknowledgment is made for permission to adapt and/or reprint original or copyrighted material, as follows:

"At the Library," from *Rhymes About Us* by Marchette Chute. Copyright © 1974 by Marchette Chute. Reprinted by permission of the author.
"Birthdays," adapted from *Little Owl, Keeper of the Trees* by Ronald and Ann Himler. Text copyright © 1974 by Ronald and Ann Himler. Reprinted by permission of Harper and Row, Publishers, Inc.

"Daniel's Duck," by Clyde Robert Bulla. Text copyright © 1979 by Clyde Robert Bulla. Reprinted by permission of Harper and Row, Publishers, Inc.
"The Elves and the Shoemaker," entire text from the book by Freya Littledale. Copyright © 1975 by Freya Littledale. Reprinted by permission of Scholastic, Inc.

Continued on page 339.

Printed in the U.S.A.

ISBN: 0-395-47699-2

DEFGHIJ-D-96543210/89

Contents

1.   Humorous Tales

Houghton Mifflin Literature
Cloudy with a Chance of Meatballs

2.   Heroic Deeds

Houghton Mifflin Literature
An Anteater Named Arthur

5.   Once Upon a Time

Houghton Mifflin Literature
Rumpelstiltskin

6. Friends

Houghton Mifflin Literature
Cherries and Cherry Pits

7. Sharing

1

Humorous Tales

The Garden

A story from *Frog and Toad Together*

Written and illustrated
by Arnold Lobel

Frog was in his garden.

Toad came walking by.

"What a fine garden you have, Frog," he said.

"Yes," said Frog. "It is very nice, but it was hard work."

"I wish I had a garden," said Toad.

"Here are some flower seeds. Plant them in the ground," said Frog, "and soon you will have a garden."

"How soon?" asked Toad.

"Quite soon," said Frog.

Toad ran home.

He planted the flower seeds.

"Now seeds," said Toad, "start growing."

Toad walked up and down a few times.

The seeds did not start to grow.

Toad put his head close to the ground
and said loudly, "Now seeds, start growing!"

Toad looked at the ground again.

The seeds did not start to grow.

Toad put his head very close to the
ground and shouted, "NOW SEEDS, START
GROWING!"

Frog came running up the path.

"What is all this noise?" he asked.

"My seeds will not grow," said Toad.

"You are shouting too much," said Frog.
"These poor seeds are afraid to grow."

"My seeds are afraid to grow?" asked
Toad.

"Of course," said Frog. "Leave them alone
for a few days. Let the sun shine on them.
Let the rain fall on them. Soon your seeds
will start to grow."

That night Toad looked out of his
window.

"Drat!" said Toad. "My seeds have not
started to grow. They must be afraid of the
dark."

Toad went out to his garden with some candles.

"I will read the seeds a story," said Toad. "Then they will not be afraid."

Toad read a long story to his seeds.

All the next day
Toad sang songs
to his seeds.

And all the next
day Toad read poems
to his seeds.

And all the next
day Toad played
music for his seeds.

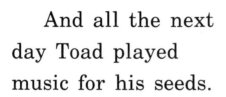

Toad looked at the ground. The seeds still did not start to grow.

"What shall I do?" cried Toad. "These must be the most frightened seeds in the whole world!"

Then Toad felt very tired, and he fell asleep.

"Toad, Toad, wake up," said Frog. "Look at your garden!"

Toad looked at his garden. Little green plants were coming up out of the ground.

"At last," shouted Toad, "my seeds have stopped being afraid to grow!"

"And now you will have a nice garden
too," said Frog.

"Yes," said Toad,
"but you were right,
Frog. It was very
hard work."

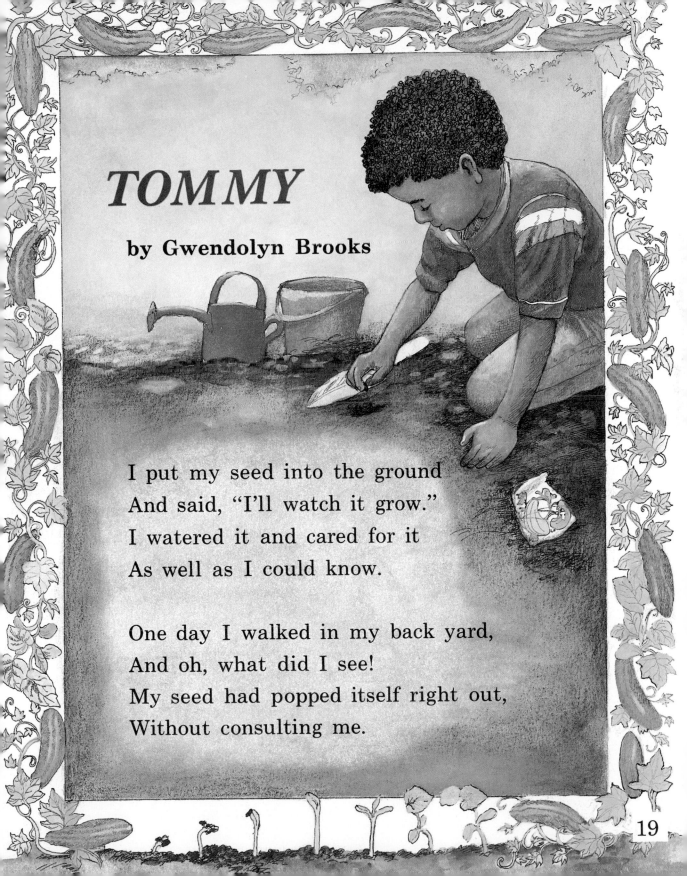

TOMMY

by Gwendolyn Brooks

I put my seed into the ground
And said, "I'll watch it grow."
I watered it and cared for it
As well as I could know.

One day I walked in my back yard,
And oh, what did I see!
My seed had popped itself right out,
Without consulting me.

THREE UP A TREE

Written and illustrated
by James Marshall

"Wow!" said Spider. "Will you look at *that*!"

Some big kids down the street had built a swell tree house.

"Can we come up?" called out Sam.

"No!" said the big kids.

"Well!" said Spider.

"Never mind," said Sam. "We'll build our own tree house."

"Let's ask Lolly to help," said Spider.

But Lolly would not help.

"I'm too busy," she said.

"You call *that* busy?" said Spider.

"Let's go," said Sam.

In no time Spider and Sam were as busy
as squirrels.

Meanwhile Lolly decided to take a little
snooze.

When Lolly woke up the tree house was
finished.

"Wow," she said. "I'll be right up."

"Oh, no," said Sam. "You didn't help."

"Oh, *please*," said Lolly.

"No!" said Spider.

"I know some good stories," said Lolly.

"Stories?" said Sam. "I love a good story."

Lolly was up the tree in a flash.

"Now tell us a story," said Sam.

"And make it good," said Spider.

"Sit down," said Lolly. "And listen
to this."

Lolly's Story

One summer evening a doll and a chicken went for a walk.

And they got lost.

"Oh, no," said the doll.

Just then a monster came around the corner.

"Oh, no," said the doll.

"Let's run!" cried the chicken.

And they ran as fast as they could.

"He's right behind us!" cried the chicken.

"Oh, no!" said the doll.

"Quick!" cried the chicken. "Let's climb that tree!"

And they did — in a jiffy.

But monsters know how to climb trees too.

"He's got us now!" cried the chicken.

"Oh, no!" cried the doll.

The monster opened his mouth.

"Will you tie my new shoes?" he said.

"Oh, yes!" said the doll.

"Not much of a story," said Spider. "The end was too sweet."

"Can you tell a better story?" said Lolly.

"Listen to this," said Spider.

Spider's Story

A chicken caught the wrong bus. She found herself in a bad part of town — the part of town where foxes live.

"Uh-oh," she said.

Quickly she pulled down her hat and waited for the next bus.

But very soon — you guessed it — a hungry fox came along and sat beside her.

His eyes were not good. But there was nothing wrong with his nose.

"I can smell that you're having chicken tonight," he said.

"Er . . ." said the chicken. "Yes, I have just been to the store."

"I *love* chicken," said the fox. "How will you cook it?"

The chicken knew she had to be clever. She did not want the fox to invite himself to dinner.

"Well," she said. "I always cook my
chicken in sour chocolate milk with lots of
pickles and rotten eggs."

"It sounds delicious," said the fox. "May I
come to dinner?"

"Let's see," said the chicken. "That will
make ten of us."

Well, *that* was too many for the fox!

He grabbed the chicken's grocery bag and
ran away.

"All for me!" he cried. "All for me!"

The poor chicken flew up into a nearby tree to wait for the next bus. (She should have done that in the first place.)

P.S. When the fox got home, he reached into the bag. But there was no chicken inside. Only the chicken's favorite food.

Can you guess what it was?

"Worms!" cried Lolly. "Worms! That story wasn't bad."

"Not bad at all," said Sam. "But now it's *my* turn."

Sam's Story

A monster woke up from a nap. He was *very* hungry.

"I want ice cream," he said. "Lots of it."

He went out to buy some. But he got lost.

"Oh, well," he said. "I'll just ask someone for help."

At that moment a fox came around the corner.

"Excuse me," said the monster.

"Help!" cried the fox. "I'm getting out of here!" And away he went.

"How rude," said the monster.

He put on the fox's hat, scarf, and glasses.

Just then a doll and a chicken came around the corner.

"Hi," said the chicken.

"Will you help me find some ice cream?" said the monster.

"If you will give us a ride in your wagon," said the chicken.

And off they went.

"Stop!" said the chicken. "This is the place for ice cream."

"Oh really?" said the monster.

"Wait here," said the doll. "We'll be right back."

In a moment they were back.

"Step on it!" said the doll. "You don't want your ice cream to melt!"

"I'll hurry!" said the monster.

"Faster!" cried the chicken.

The monster ran as fast as he could.
Soon they came to a big tree.

"This is where we live," said the doll.

And they all climbed up the tree.

The doll and the chicken opened their
bags. But there was no ice cream inside.
There was only money.

"Oh, no!" said the monster. "You are bank
robbers!"

The monster took off his hat, scarf, and
glasses.

The doll and the chicken were scared out
of their wits.

"Help, help!" they cried. "Let's get out of
here!"

And they ran as fast as their little legs
could carry them.

The monster returned the money to the bank. As a reward he was given all the ice cream he could eat. And there was *lots* of it!

"My story was better," said Lolly.

"No, mine was," said Spider.

"No, mine!" said Sam.

"Let's hear them again," said Lolly.

And they did.

Houghton Mifflin Literature

You have just read two funny stories.
Here is another one — *Cloudy With a
Chance of Meatballs*, by Judi Barrett.

Grandpa tells a tale about a town
called Chewandswallow where the weather
is so good you can eat it!

Heroic Deeds

43

JASPER
and the
Hero Business

by Betty Horvath
Illustrated by Eric Jon Nones

Jasper lived in the house on the corner. It was a busy corner. All day long people passed by, hurrying to work, hurrying home again.

Jasper didn't hurry. He didn't have any place to go. Sometimes he didn't have anything to do. He watched the people pass by.

Sometimes they stopped and talked to him. They asked him questions.

There was one question that EVERYBODY asked him. "What are you going to be when you grow up?"

"I'm going to be a hero," Jasper said.

And then they laughed.

"Wait and see," thought Jasper. "Someday I am going to be a big hero. I will have my picture in the paper."

"OK, Jasper the Hero," said his brother Paul, "I have a job for you."

"This is no job for a hero," said Jasper. But he carried out the garbage anyway.

Then he went back to sit under his tree and wait for something brave to do.

A fire engine went clanging by.

"There goes a hero," said Jasper. "Off to do brave deeds and help people in trouble."

That night the newspaper had a picture of a fireman. He was carrying a baby down a ladder. Jasper cut the picture out of the paper.

That's the way his hero board began.

Every time Jasper read about someone being brave he pinned the story to the board on his bedroom wall.

"Someday," said Jasper, "my picture will be up there, too."

He was saving a place for it.

"There is never anything dangerous going on around here," said Jasper.

"That's good," said his mother. "Let's keep it that way."

Jasper took Rover for a walk.

Then he saw somebody running down the street.

"Maybe there has been a robbery," Jasper thought. "Maybe this is a thief coming! When he gets closer Rover and I can catch him. Maybe Rover will even bite him!"

But then the runner got closer. Jasper saw it was Mr. Brown out doing his jogging. He patted Rover's head.

Rover wagged his tail.

"Some adventure!" thought Jasper.

He turned the corner. Right there on the ground was a piece of paper. It was money!

"If I can't be brave," said Jasper, "it's good to be rich."

When he got to the next corner, he heard somebody crying. It sounded like someone was in trouble. Maybe even in danger!

"Here's my chance to be a hero," said Jasper.

But then he saw the little boy. He was standing in front of Jasper's house. Not even bleeding or anything.

"Are you lost?" Jasper asked. "Can I take you home?"

Jasper could see it now. Headlines in the paper. HERO RETURNS LOST CHILD.

"No," sobbed the little boy, *"I'm* not lost. My money's lost."

Jasper sighed. "I found some money," he said. "I guess it's yours."

The little boy took it. He didn't say anything. He just watched Jasper and Rover go into the house.

"Maybe I'm going about this hero business all wrong," thought Jasper.

"Do you know any heroes?" he asked his mother.

"Look out the window," said his mother. "There is a hero coming up the walk this very minute."

Jasper ran to the window.

"That's just father," he said. "I never knew he was a hero."

"There are all kinds of heroes," said his mother. "Your father worked hard today to earn money to pay the rent and the grocery bill. Maybe he would rather have gone fishing. It is a lucky family who has a hero like your father."

"Then I will put his picture on my hero
board," said Jasper.

So Jasper found a picture of his father.
Then he pinned his mother's picture up
beside it.

But there was still the empty place
where his picture belonged. He was getting
older every minute. Another day was almost
gone. Jasper wasn't a hero yet.

While they were eating dinner, the doorbell rang.

Jasper's father came back carrying a bunch of flowers.

"These are for you," he said.

"Jasper has a girl!" said Paul.

"No," said his father, "it was a little boy. He said Jasper gave him some money."

"Oh, *him*!" said Jasper. "I *found* some money, but it was his. I just gave it back to him."

Nobody said anything for a minute. Then Paul said, "I bet that little boy thinks Jasper is a hero."

"Who, me? A hero?"

"Sure," said Paul. "If somebody *thinks* you're a hero, you *are* one. It is time to pin your picture on the hero board."

Paul helped him pin the picture up. Under it they wrote "Jasper the Hero." The board was finished now. There was no more empty space.

"Now that you are a hero," said Paul, "what are you going to be next?"

"You don't ever stop being a hero," said Jasper. "But maybe I'll be something else, too. I think I'll be a hero *and* work on being a doctor. What are you going to do?"

"Me?" asked Paul. "I'm going to be busy trying not to get sick!"

UNTIL I SAW THE SEA

by Lilian Moore

Until I saw the sea
I did not know
that wind
could wrinkle water so.

I never knew
that sun
could splinter
a whole sea of blue.

Nor
did I know before,
a sea breathes in and out
upon a shore.

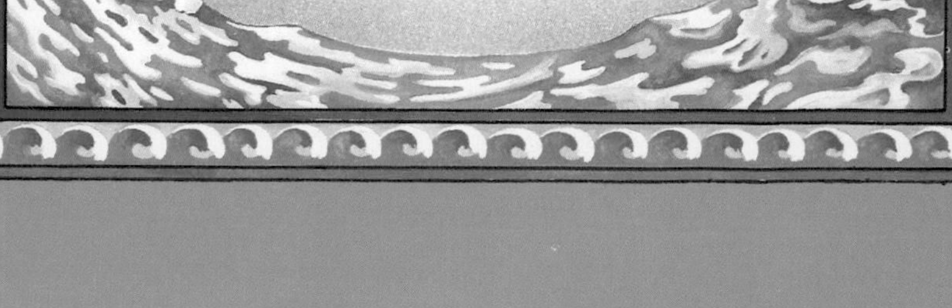

A Thousand Pails of Water

by Ronald Roy

Illustrated by Mai Vo-Dinh

Yukio lived in a village where people fished and hunted whales to make their living. Yukio's father, too, was a whale hunter.

"Why do you kill the whales, Father?" Yukio asked. "Suki's father works in the market and his hands are never red from blood."

"Hunting the whale is all I know," his father answered.

But Yukio did not understand.

Yukio went to his grandfather and asked again. "Why does my father kill the whales?"

"Your father does what he must do," his grandfather said. "Let him be, little one, and ask your questions of the sea."

So Yukio went to the sea.

Small creatures scurried from under his feet in the tide pools. Large scavenger birds screamed at him from the sky, "Bring us food!"

Then Yukio saw a whale that had become lodged between some rocks and was left behind when the tide went out.

The large tail flukes beat the sand, helplessly. The eye, as big as Yukio's hand, rolled in fright.

Yukio knew that the whale would not live long out of the sea.

"I will help you, sir," he said.

But how? The whale was huge, like a temple.

Yukio raced to the water's edge. Was the tide coming in or going out? In, he decided, by the way the little fingers of foam climbed higher with each new wave.

The sun was hot on Yukio's back as he stood looking at the whale.

Yukio filled his pail with water and threw it over the great head.

"You are so big and my pail is so small!" he cried. "But I will throw a thousand pails of water over you before I stop."

The second pail went on the head as well, and the third and the fourth. But Yukio knew he must wet every part of the whale or it would die in the sun.

Yukio made many trips to the sea for water, counting as he went. He threw four pails on the body, then four on the tail, and then three on the head.

There was a little shade on one side of the big gray prisoner. Yukio sat there, out of breath, his heart pounding.

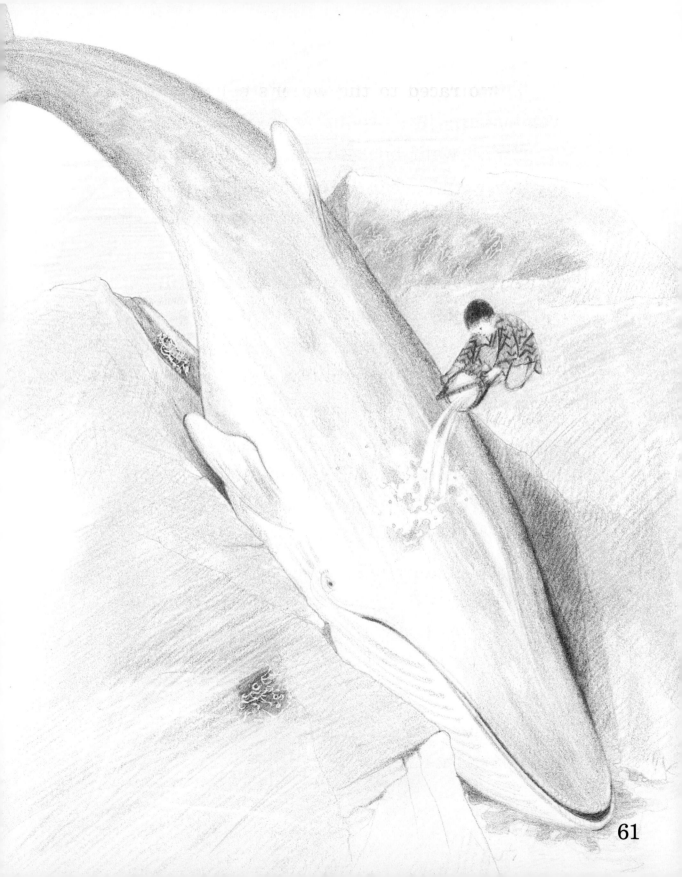

Then he looked in the whale's eye and remembered his promise.

Yukio went back to the sea and stooped to fill his pail. How many had he filled so far? He had lost count. But he knew he must not stop.

Yukio fell, the precious water spilling from his pail. He cried, and his tears disappeared into the sand.

A wave touched his foot, as if to say, "Get up and carry more water. I am coming, but I am very slow."

Yukio filled his pail over and over. His back hurt, and his arms — but he threw and threw.

He fell again, but this time he did not get up.

Yukio felt himself being lifted.

"You have worked hard, little one. Now let us help."

Yukio's grandfather lay him in the shade of one of the rocks. Yukio watched his grandfather throw his first pail of water and go for another.

"Hurry!" Yukio wanted to scream, for his grandfather was old and walked slowly.

Then Yukio heard the voices. His father and the village people were running toward the sea. They carried pails and buckets and anything that would hold water.

Some of the villagers removed their jackets and soaked them in the sea. These they placed on the whale's burning skin. Soon the whale was wet all over.

Slowly the sea came closer and closer. At last it covered the huge tail. The village people ran back and forth carrying water, shouting to each other. Yukio knew the whale would be saved.

Yukio's father came and stood by him. "Thank you, Father," Yukio said, "for bringing the village people to help."

"You are strong and good," his father said. "But to save a whale many hands must carry the water."

Now the whale was moving with each new wave. Suddenly a great one lifted him free of the rocks. He was still for a moment, then, with a flip of his tail, swam out to sea.

The villagers watched silently, as the whale swam farther and farther from their shore. Then they turned and walked toward the village.

Except for Yukio, who was asleep in the arms of his father.

He had carried a thousand pails of water, and he was tired.

THE LIFE CYCLE

OF THE

WHALE

by Paula Z. Hogan

Illustrated by Meg Kelleher Aubrey

Humpback whales live in the sea but are not fish. They breathe air and stay warm in the coldest weather.

Blubber is a thick layer of fat. It keeps the whales warm. When they have no food, whales can live off their blubber.

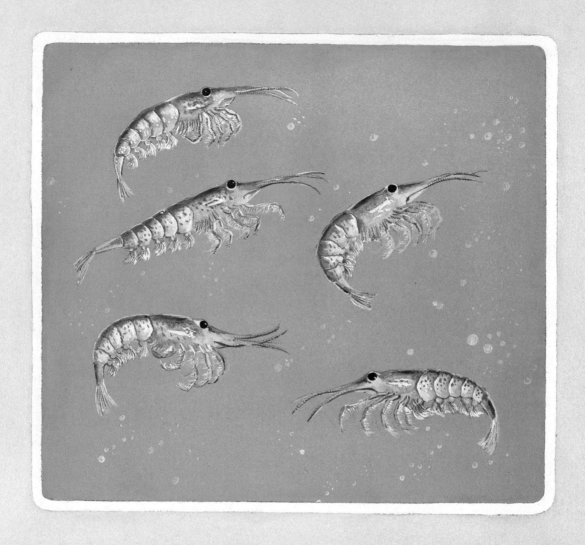

Most great whales don't need teeth. They
eat very small animals called krill.

Krill live in icy water near the North and
South Poles. Whales feed all summer long.
Their mouths can hold a ton of krill!

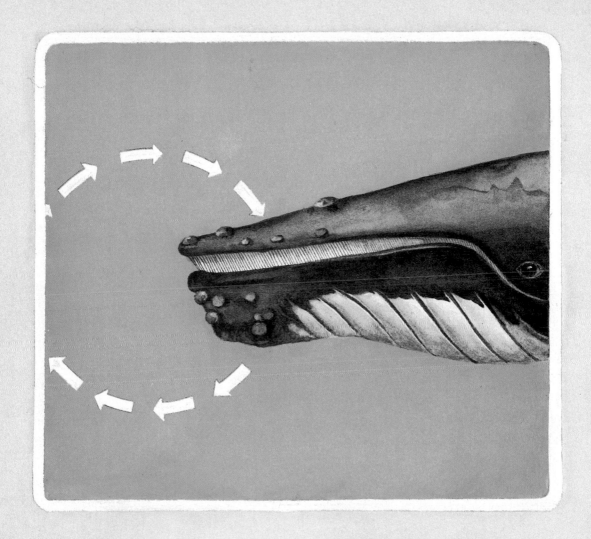

Whales can't see or smell very well. How do they find food?

Whales make a clicking sound, then listen for the echo. The echo tells them where to find krill.

Side fins work to steer, dive, and stop. The tail fins push the whale along. Whales like to jump out of the water and fall back with a splash.

Whales can stay underwater a long time. Then they stay above water for a few minutes before diving down again.

They breathe through a hole on the top of their heads. When they blow out, a small cloud forms.

In winter whales swim to warmer waters. They go together in large herds. Year after year each herd comes back to the same place.

Baby whales are born in early winter. Like many land animals, mother whales give milk to their babies.

By summer the babies have grown a layer of blubber. Then the herd heads for colder water to eat krill.

Every year there are fewer whales. Many are hunted for their blubber and meat. Soon there may be no whales at all.

Other animals live in the sea, breathe air, and give milk to their babies. Some are dolphins, porpoises, and narwhals. None of these grow bigger than whales. Whales are the biggest animals of all.

narwhal

dolphin

porpoise

by
Peter and Connie Roop
pictures by
Peter E. Hanson

Houghton Mifflin Literature

You have read about some heroes.
Keep the Lights Burning, Abbie by
Peter and Connie Roop, is about a
young hero in Maine.

Find out what happens when it is
Abbie's job to care for the lighthouse lamps.

3

Wishing
and
Wishing
Again

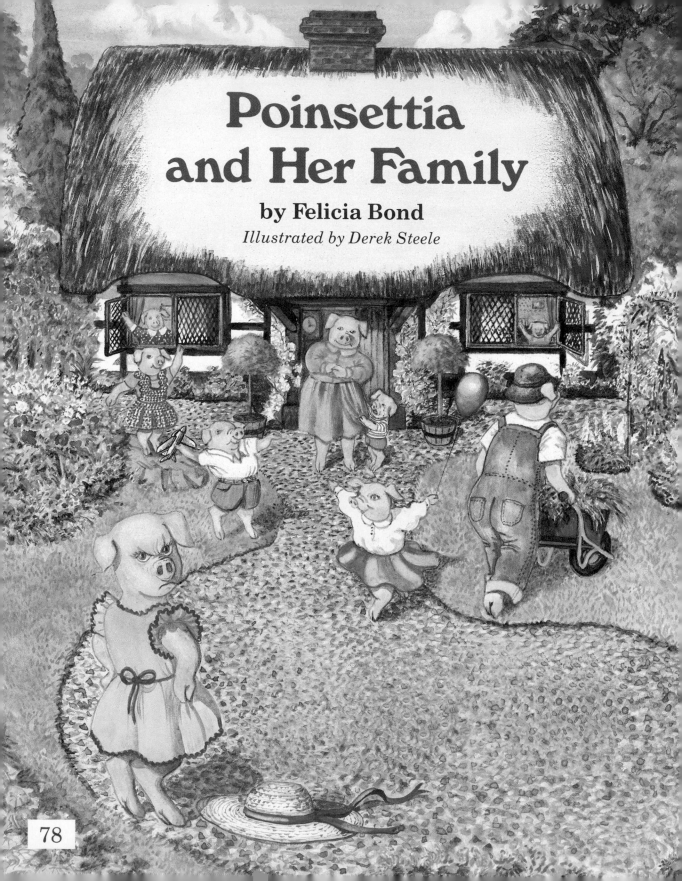

Poinsettia
and Her Family

by Felicia Bond

Illustrated by Derek Steele

Poinsettia had six brothers and sisters, a mother, and a father.

They lived in a fine, old house surrounded by hydrangea bushes and lilac hedges, which Poinsettia's mother would occasionally cut for a nice effect in the dining room.

There was pachysandra in which to play hide-and-seek in the early evenings of summer, and a rock out front to sit on.

Inside, there was a red leather window seat for reading in the late afternoon sun, and a bathroom with balloon-pink wallpaper. Poinsettia thought it a perfect house.

One day, Poinsettia came home from the library with her favorite book, a book about a little, spotted circus horse who danced. Poinsettia had read it five times before, but she was looking forward to it all the same.

She trotted past her mother in the garden and her father in the kitchen, and headed straight for the red leather window seat.

If the sun was coming in the window just right, it would spread like warm butter across the pages of her book. Poinsettia walked a little faster, patting her pocket to make sure it held the cherry tart she had bought for just this occasion.

The sun was coming in the window just right, but it was spreading like warm butter across the fat, little body of Julius, the third from the youngest, who was already curled up on the soft red leather.

"I will go to the rock in the front yard," Poinsettia grunted, "where I can read my book in peace."

But the rock could hardly be seen for all the piglets lying about. "Like a bunch of seals," Poinsettia snorted.

She stomped off toward the balloon-pink
bathroom, where the tub was just right for
reading. But there, up to her chins in water,
was Chick Pea, who said she hadn't washed
her feet yet.

"This house would be perfect except for
one thing," Poinsettia fumed. "There are too
many of us in it! It is not possible to go
anywhere without running into a brother or
a sister, a mother or a father!"

That night, Poinsettia was very nasty.
She pinched a brother, stepped on a sister,
and yelled louder than both of them put
together.

She did more things and worse things, and it was only seven o'clock.

Poinsettia was sent to bed early that night for general misbehavior.

The next day, Poinsettia's father announced to the whole family that they were moving. "We will look for a new house," he said. "This one is too small for us."

"Oh, no, it's not," Poinsettia thought. "It's the family that's too big." But she kept her thoughts to herself and vowed not to go with them.

When the family left, Poinsettia lay low in the pachysandra. Nobody noticed. The car seemed full.

She lay there a long time, just in case they came back. They didn't.

"Good!" Poinsettia said and, clutching her book close to her, ran straight for the red leather window seat.

The light had never been more buttery, nor the leather as warm. Poinsettia read two pages there, then ran to the rock in the front yard. The rock had never felt more solid.

Poinsettia read six more pages. But a wind was whipping up, and it was even starting to snow.

Poinsettia ran inside.

She warmed herself in a deliciously hot
bath. She read four pages, then spent an
hour staring dreamily at the wallpaper. It
had never looked pinker, and neither had
Poinsettia.

"I'm a pig in bliss," she gurgled.

Poinsettia let the water out of the tub.

The snow came down harder, and
Poinsettia fell asleep. She dreamed about
the dancing circus horse.

It snowed all that afternoon and into the evening. By the time it was dark, Poinsettia had read her book eighteen times. She wrapped herself in an old blanket and looked for something to eat. What little food there was she ate cold.

"The house is not as it used to be," she said aloud quietly.

"What I need is a rope! If I had a rope, I could make a tent with this blanket. I could tie the rope to two doorknobs and put the blanket over it. My tent would be a house inside a house. What a good idea."

Poinsettia searched everywhere for a bit of rope. All she found was a frayed piece of string that was barely long enough for anything.

But in the farthest corner of a dark, dark closet, Poinsettia found something else. It was a photograph, an old photograph of her family. Poinsettia remembered taking it herself.

This was too much for Poinsettia.

With the point of her hoof, she very carefully made a little hole in the top of the photograph. Through the hole she threaded the string she had found. On each end she made a knot.

"This is all I have left of my family!" Poinsettia cried, and cried, and cried.

"Poinsettia!" a small voice called. "Poinsettia!"

Poinsettia nearly fainted dead away.

There were her six brothers and sisters, her mother and her father, all squashed and crowded together and smiling from ear to ear!

"We would have been back sooner," Poinsettia's father said, "but the car got stuck in the snow. It's a good thing there are so many of us. We all got out and pushed."

"Pierre counted everyone, but he counted wrong because he's only three," said Petunia, the oldest.

"I don't know why we didn't notice right away that you were missing," Julius said, "because everything was so peaceful."

"The whole time we were gone, Poinsettia," her mother said, "we talked about what a wonderful house this is. It is our home. Perhaps we don't need as much room as we thought."

"Maybe not," Poinsettia said.

And shoulder to shoulder, elbow to elbow, all squashed and crowded together, they spent the rest of that night, and many other nights together. . . as together as nine pigs could be. . . in their fine, old house.

AT THE LIBRARY

by Marchette Chute

This is a lovely place to be.
  The books are everywhere,
And I can read them here, or take
  Them home and read them there.
It is a kind of secret place
  Where I can enter in
And no one tells me where to stop
  Or where I should begin.

The books sit waiting on their shelves,
  As friendly as can be,
And since I am a borrower
  They all belong to me.

Daniel's Duck

by Clyde Robert Bulla

Illustrated by Nancy Edwards Calder

Jeff and Daniel were brothers. They lived in a cabin on a mountain in Tennessee.

Jeff had a good knife. He could carve with it. He could carve things out of wood. He made a dish. He made a cup and a spoon.

His mother and father were proud.

"Some day," they said, "you may be as good as Henry Pettigrew."

Henry Pettigrew lived in the valley. They had never seen him, but they had seen his work. He was a wood-carver. Some said he was the best wood-carver in Tennessee.

Henry Pettigrew carved animals. His birds looked as if they could fly. His horses looked as if they could run. All his animals looked real.

Jeff and his brother Daniel had seen some of them in town.

"I want to carve an animal," said Jeff. "I want to carve a deer or a turkey or a bear like Henry Pettigrew's. But animals are hard to do."

"I want to carve an animal, too," said Daniel.

"You're not old enough," said Jeff.

"Yes, I am," said Daniel. "I could carve one if I had a good knife and some wood."

"It takes more than a good knife and some wood," said Jeff.

"What does it take?" asked Daniel.

"You have to know how," said Jeff. "It's hard to carve an animal."

"I know how," said Daniel.

"Let's see if you do," said his father.

He gave Daniel a knife like Jeff's. He gave him a block of wood.

It was winter. The nights were long.

"This is a good time to sit by the fire and carve," said Jeff. "I'm going to make something for the spring fair."

Every spring there was a fair in the valley. It was time for people to meet after the long winter. It was a time to show things that they had made. Sometimes they sold what they had made. Sometimes they traded with one another.

Father knew how to make Indian moccasins. On winter nights he made moccasins to take to the fair.

Mother cut pieces of cloth. She sewed them together to make a quilt.

"This will be a warm quilt for somebody's bed," she said. "I'll take it to the fair."

"I'm going to make a box for the fair," said Jeff. "I'm going to carve little moons on the lid." He said to his brother, "You haven't done anything with your block of wood. What are you going to make?"

"I have to think," said Daniel.

Days went by. Then he began to carve.

"What are you making?" asked Jeff.

"You'll see," said Daniel.

One night Jeff looked at what Daniel was carving. He saw a neck and a head. He saw a wing.

"Now I see," he said. "It's a bird."

"It's a duck," said Daniel.

"You're not doing it right," said Jeff. "Its head is on backward."

"I want it that way," said Daniel. "My duck is looking back."

"That's no way to do it," said Jeff.

Father said, "Let him do it his way."

Spring came. It was time for the fair. Mother had made her quilt. Father had made three pairs of moccasins. Jeff's box was done.

"It took a long time," he said.

"My duck took a long time, too," said Daniel.

"Are you sure you want to take it to the fair?" asked Jeff.

"Yes," said Daniel.

They went down the mountain in a wagon. Father drove the horses. They drove into town. There were people everywhere. Everyone had come to the fair.

Father took the quilt and the moccasins. He took Jeff's box and Daniel's duck. He left them at the hall. The hall was a long house in the middle of town.

"This is where the show will be," said Father. "People are getting it ready now."

They walked down the street. They saw the river. They talked with friends.

Father said, "The hall is open."

They went to the show. There were pictures that people had made. There were quilts and rugs and baskets. There were dolls. There were coonskin caps.

"Where are the wood carvings?" asked Daniel.

"Over here," said Jeff.

They went to the end of the hall. The carvings were there on tables. On a small table was a carved deer. It was so beautiful that people were quiet when they looked at it. Everyone knew it had been done by Henry Pettigrew.

On a big table were the carvings that others had done.

"I see my box," said Jeff.

"I see my duck," said Daniel.

Many people were looking at the carvings. They were laughing.

"What are they laughing at?" asked Daniel.

Jeff didn't answer.

Someone said, "Look at the duck!"

Someone else said, "That duck is so funny!"

More people came to look. More people were laughing. Now Daniel knew. They were laughing at his duck. He wanted to go away. He wanted to hide.

Then he was angry. He went to the table. He picked up his duck and ran with it. He ran out of the hall.

Someone was running after him. He ran faster. He came to the river.

He started to throw the duck as far as he could. But he could not throw it. A man had hold of his arm.

The man asked, "What are you doing with that duck?"

"I'm going to throw it in the river!" said Daniel.

"You can't do that," said the man.

"I can if I want to," said Daniel. "It's mine."

"Did you make it?" asked the man.

"Yes," said Daniel.

"Why were you going to throw it away?" asked the man.

"They all laughed at it," said Daniel.

"Listen to me," said the man. "There are different ways of laughing. The people *liked* your duck. They laughed because they liked it."

"No. It's ugly," said Daniel.

"It *isn't* ugly. It's a good duck. It made me feel happy. That's why I laughed."

The man was not laughing now. "You're hot and tired," he said. "Come and rest in the shade."

They sat under a tree.

"Would you sell your duck?" asked the man.

"Who would buy it?" asked Daniel.

"I might think of someone," said the man.

A boy and girl came up to them. "How are you, Mr. Pettigrew?" they asked.

"I'm fine," said the man.

The boy and girl went on.

Daniel said, "You're Henry Pettigrew!"

"Yes," said the man. "I'm a wood-carver, too."

"I know that," said Daniel. He was holding his duck. He looked down at it. It wasn't ugly. It was a good duck. Henry Pettigrew had said so, and he knew.

"I saw your deer," said Daniel.

"I made it last winter," said the man. "I've made lots of things. My house is full of them."

Daniel said, "I wish — " and then he stopped.

"What do you wish?" asked the man.

"I wish I could see the things you've made," said Daniel.

"I'll show them to you," said the man. "Maybe today, after the fair. Shall we go back to the fair now?"

"Yes," said Daniel.

They got up. The man was looking at the duck.

"Will you sell it to me?" he asked.

"No," said Daniel. He held the duck a little longer. Then he gave it to Henry Pettigrew.

JOSEFINA FEBRUARY

WRITTEN AND ILLUSTRATED BY

EVALINE NESS

Not long ago on a high hill in Haiti there lived a little girl named Josefina February. Josefina lived with her grandfather, Mr. February, in a house that had one room, bamboo walls and a banana leaf roof.

In front of their house stood an enormous Silk-cotton tree in which Josefina had her private sitting room.

From her room in the tree she could watch
the sea a mile away, and the market place
which was halfway to the sea.

In back of their house was the grove, surrounded by a cactus fence. In the grove there were oranges, breadfruit, bananas and yams; avocados, mangoes, pineapples and beans. Poppies, which grew everywhere, covered the ground and poinsettias ringed round the trunks of the calabash trees.

Early every morning Josefina and her
grandfather went to the grove and picked the
fruit which had ripened overnight. They carried
the fruit in baskets on their heads and walked
down the hill to the market place. With the
money they earned from the fruit they sold,
they bought candles and matches, salt and
soap, and sometimes calico. Mr. February
always gave Josefina a penny or two to spend
as she pleased.

Josefina loved the market place. There was so much to see and smell and hear. People, baskets, hats and mats were all mixed in with coffee beans, sisal and rice. Bananas and yams, meat and beans boiled in big black cauldrons over charcoal fires. There were sugar-cane candies and coconuts. There were beads, ribbons, combs and shoes; calabash bowls and wicker chairs, and goats and oranges everywhere. Church bells rang, donkeys brayed and children blew bamboo trumpets.

One morning, instead of going to market, Mr. February went to work all day in Mr. Hippolyte's sugar-cane fields. He told Josefina to play at home — but Josefina had other plans.

That day was her grandfather's birthday and Josefina wanted to buy him a pair of real leather shoes. She decided to go to the market alone. If she could sell one basket of fruit she would have enough money, with the pennies she had saved, to buy the shoes.

113

After her grandfather left, Josefina took her basket and went to the grove. While she was picking the oranges, mangoes, bananas and yams, she heard a strange sound. It seemed to come from the coffee berry bush. Josefina looked behind the bush and saw a little black burro, with a fringe of brown hair on top of his head that looked like a cap. His legs were so wobbly he could hardly stand and his ears looked as long as his legs.

Josefina picked him up and held him close. The little burro folded his soft ears and put his head under Josefina's chin. She decided to call him Cap.

She wondered if Cap belonged to someone. How she wished he belonged to her! She would teach him clever tricks. She would play games with him. And when he was older, she would ride on his back to the sea.

Josefina was so busy dreaming of the future, it was noon before she remembered the fruit she had picked to take to the market.

She couldn't bear the thought of leaving
Cap, so she decided to take him with her.

As she stood there in the noonday sun,
Josefina suddenly felt cold. What if Cap
belonged to the very first person she met?
Would that be worse than the very last?
First, last, last or first, it would be the same: if
Cap belonged to someone else, he couldn't belong
to her.

But perhaps he was like Josefina who had no mother, no father, no sister, no brother. Cap might not even have a grandfather. He might, just possibly, belong to no one in the whole world except Josefina!

Somehow she felt warmer, so she put her basket on her head, picked up Cap and started down the hill.

As she passed the cemetery, the first person she met was Lilly, the tallest, haughtiest girl on the hill. Lilly had a bandanna full of bananas on her head. "Pardon me, Lilly," Josefina said. "As you can see, I have a baby burro here. Does he belong to you?"

Lilly swept by without a word.

When Lilly had gone, Josefina whispered to Cap, "Well, anyway, it wasn't the *first* person."

She met no one else until she reached the bottom of the hill. There she saw a little girl and her brother who were selling oranges by the roadside.

Josefina went up to them and said, "Pardon me. As you can see, I have a baby burro here. What do you think of him?"

The girl and her brother, as if they were one, said, "We wish he belonged to us!"

Josefina smiled and continued along the road. Suddenly she heard a croak, a cackle and a screech. She turned around and saw an old woman with three blackbirds. When Josefina asked, "Pardon me, have you lost a baby burro?" the old woman said not a word, but the three blackbirds cackled and croaked, "Not we not we not we!"

Josefina felt light with happiness. So far, no one belonged to Cap!

Soon she came to a house that looked like a kite on a string. Two sisters named Yvette and Yvonne were standing on the porch. Josefina walked up to them and asked politely, "Miss Yvette and Miss Yvonne, would you know anyone who might have lost a baby burro? This burro here?"

119

Yvette and Yvonne smiled at Josefina and simply said, "No, dear."

Josefina hugged Cap and hurried on to the market place. When she got there she could hardly believe her eyes. The market place was empty! All the people had taken their wares and gone home to supper.

Josefina didn't know what to do. She was happy and sad at the same time. Now Cap belonged to her, but she had not sold the fruit and she had no real leather shoes to give to her grandfather for his birthday.

She turned away from the market place and started to walk slowly home. As she passed Mr. Hippolyte's sugar-cane fields, she was surprised to hear her name called. It was Mr. Hippolyte himself leaning on the fence with his big straw hat resting on his nose.

Josefina tried to smile, but instead she started to cry. She cried so hard she thought she would never be able to stop long enough to tell Mr. Hippolyte her terrible trouble.

Mr. Hippolyte just waited. At last Josefina wiped away her tears and told him her story.

Mr. Hippolyte looked at Josefina a long time. Then he said, "It just happens that I have a new pair of real leather shoes. Would you consider trading Cap for the shoes?"

It was Josefina's turn to look at Mr.
Hippolyte a long time. Then she nodded her
head. She was afraid to speak for fear she
would cry again.

While she waited for Mr. Hippolyte to return with the shoes, Josefina did cry a little more.

She made two neat braids in Cap's mane and tied them with the ribbons from her hair. She kissed Cap's nose and told him to be good. She promised Cap she would never, never forget him.

When Josefina got home it was almost dark. She cooked ham and yams in a big pot and cut up all the fruit from her basket for dessert.

She had just put the shoes in the middle of the table when Mr. February walked in. He stood there and smiled at Josefina. And Josefina stood there and smiled back.

Then Mr. February put on his real leather shoes and kissed Josefina on top of her head.

Mr. February and Josefina ate the birthday supper in silence.

They had almost finished when Mr. February said, "Poor Mr. Hippolyte. He has a responsibility, not a very big one, but he thinks he cannot handle it alone. He wondered if you would like to take care of it for him."

Josefina stared at her grandfather. Mr. Hippolyte had a responsibility! She started to speak but before she could say a word, the door slowly opened.

And in wobbled a little black burro, fringed on top, with ribbons in his mane.

You have just read some stories about wishing. What would you do if you weren't happy about a wish that came true? Would you wish again?

Find out what Scamp the dog wishes in *The Whingdingdilly* by Bill Peet.

Nobody's Perfect

GREGORY,
the Terrible Eater

by Mitchell Sharmat

Illustrated by Jose Aruego and Ariane Dewey

Once there was a goat named Gregory.

Gregory liked to jump from rock to rock, kick his legs into the air, and butt his head against walls.

"I'm an average goat," said Gregory.

But Gregory was not an average goat.

Gregory was a terrible eater.

Every time he sat down to eat with his mother and father, he knew he was in for trouble.

131

"Would you like a tin can, Gregory?"
asked Mother Goat.

"No, thanks," said Gregory.

"How about a nice box, a piece of rug,
and a bottle cap?" asked Father Goat.

"Baaaaaa," said Gregory unhappily.

"Well, I think this is a meal fit for a goat," said Mother Goat, as she chewed on an old shoe.

"It certainly is," said Father Goat, as he ate a shirt, buttons and all. "I don't know why you're such a fussy eater, Gregory."

"I'm not fussy," said Gregory. "I just want fruits, vegetables, eggs, fish, bread, and butter. Good stuff like that."

Mother Goat stopped eating the shoe. "Now what kind of food is *that*, Gregory?" she said.

"It's what I like," said Gregory.

"It's revolting," said Father Goat. He wiped his mouth with his napkin.

After Gregory was excused from the table, Father Goat said, "Gregory is such a terrible eater."

"I wonder what's wrong with him," said Mother Goat.

Mother and Father Goat ate their evening newspaper in silence.

The next morning Mother and Father Goat were enjoying a pair of pants and a coat for breakfast.

Gregory came to the table.

"Good morning, Gregory," said Father and Mother Goat.

"Good morning," said Gregory. "May I have some orange juice, cereal, and bananas for breakfast, please."

"Oh, no!" Mother Goat said. "Do have some of this nice coat."

"Take a bite out of these pants," said Father Goat.

"Baaaaaa," said Gregory. And he left the table.

Father Goat threw down his napkin. "That does it!" he said. "Gregory just isn't eating right. We must take him to the doctor."

Father and Mother Goat took Gregory to the doctor. Dr. Ram was munching on a few pieces of cardboard.

"What seems to be the trouble?" he asked.

"Gregory is a terrible eater," said Mother Goat. "We've offered him the best — shoes, boxes, magazines, tin cans, coats, pants. But all he wants are fruits, vegetables, eggs, fish, orange juice, and other horrible things."

"What do you have to say about all of this, Gregory?" asked Dr. Ram.

"I want what I like," said Gregory.

"Makes sense," said Dr. Ram. He turned to Mother and Father Goat. "I've treated picky eaters before," he said. "They have to develop a taste for good food slowly. Try giving Gregory one new food each day until he eats everything."

That night for dinner Mother Goat gave Gregory spaghetti and a shoelace in tomato sauce.

"Not too bad," said Gregory.

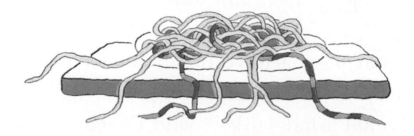

The next day she gave him string beans and a rubber heel cut into small pieces.

"The meal was good and rubbery," said Gregory.

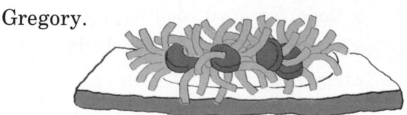

The day after that, Mother Goat said, "We have your favorite today. Vegetable soup. But there is one condition. You also have to eat the can."

"Okay," said Gregory. "What's for dessert?"

"Ice cream," said Father Goat. "But you
have to eat the box, too."

"Yummy," said Gregory.

"I'm proud of you," said Father Goat.
"You're beginning to eat like a goat."

"I'm learning to like everything," said
Gregory.

One evening Father Goat asked, "Has
anyone seen my striped necktie?"

"Not since breakfast," said Mother Goat.
"Come to think of it, I haven't seen my
sewing basket today. I left it in the living
room after supper last night."

Father Goat turned to Gregory. "Gregory, have you been eating between meals?"

"Yes," said Gregory. "I can't help it. Now I like everything."

"Well," said Mother Goat, "it's all right to eat like a goat, but you shouldn't eat like a pig."

"Oh," said Gregory.

After Gregory went to bed, Mother Goat said, "I'm afraid Gregory will eat my clothes hamper."

"Yes, and then my tool kit will be next," said Father Goat. "He's eating too much. We'll have to do something about it."

The next evening, just before supper, Mother and Father Goat went to the town dump.

They brought home eight flat tires, a three-foot piece of barber pole, a broken violin, and half a car. They piled everything in front of Gregory's sandbox.

When Gregory came home for supper he said, "What's all that stuff in the yard?"

"Your supper," said Father Goat.

"It all looks good," said Gregory.

Gregory ate the tires and the violin.
Then he slowly ate the barber pole. But
when he started in on the car, he said, "I've
got a stomachache. I have to lie down."

Gregory went to his room.

"I think Gregory ate too much junk," said
Father Goat.

"Let's hope so," said Mother Goat.

142

All night Gregory tossed and twisted and moaned and groaned.

The next morning he went down for breakfast.

"What would you like for breakfast today, Gregory?" asked Father Goat.

"Scrambled eggs and two pieces of waxed paper and a glass of orange juice," said Gregory.

"That sounds just about right," said Mother Goat.

And it was.

Katy No-Pocket

Story by Emmy Payne

Pictures by H. A. Rey

Big tears rolled down Katy Kangaroo's brown face. Poor Katy was crying because she didn't have a pocket like other mother kangaroos. Freddy was Katy Kangaroo's little boy and he needed a pocket to ride in. All grown-up kangaroos take awfully big hops and little kangaroos, like Freddy, get left far behind unless their mothers have nice pockets to carry them in.

And poor Katy didn't have any pocket at all.

Katy Kangaroo cried just thinking about it, and Freddy cried, too.

Then, all of a sudden, Katy had a wonderful idea! It was so wonderful she jumped six feet up in the air.

The idea was this. Other animal mothers had children and they didn't have any pockets. She'd go and ask one of them how they carried their babies!

Freddy looked all around to see whom to ask and Katy looked all around to see, too. And what they both saw were two bubbles rising up from the river right beside them.

"Mrs. Crocodile!" said Katy, feeling lots better already. "*She* hasn't any pocket. Let's ask her!"

A lot of big muddy bubbles came up through the water and then Mrs. Crocodile stuck her head up and opened her *enormous* mouth and smiled.

"Why, Katy Kangaroo! What can I do for you today?"

"Please, Mrs. Crocodile, I am so sad," said Katy. "I have no pocket and Freddy has to walk wherever we go and he gets so tired. Oh dear, oh dear!"

And she started to cry again.

The crocodile began to cry, too, and then she said, "B–b–but — What — what can *I* do?"

"You can tell me how to carry Freddy," said Katy. "How do you carry little Catherine Crocodile? Oh, do *please* tell me."

"Why, I carry her on my back, of course!" said Mrs. Crocodile.

She was so surprised that anyone shouldn't know that she forgot to cry any more.

Katy was pleased. She said, "Thank you," and as soon as she got to a good squatting-down place, she squatted and said, "Now, Freddy, climb on my back. After this it will be so simple — no trouble at all."

But it wasn't simple.

In the first place, Freddy could not crawl up onto her back because his knees stuck out. He couldn't hang on because his front legs were too short. And when he did manage to hang on for a few minutes and Katy gave a long hop, he fell off — bump, bang — with a terrific thump.

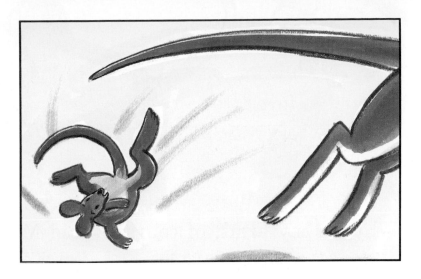

So Katy saw that she couldn't carry her baby on her back.

Katy and Freddy sat down again and thought and thought.

"I know! I'll ask Mrs. Monkey. I'm sure she can help me."

So Katy and Freddy set off for the forest and very soon they found Mrs. Monkey. She had her young son, Jocko, with her and Katy Kangaroo hurried so to catch up with them that she was almost out of breath. But, finally, she managed to squeak, "Please, Mrs. Monkey, how do you carry Jocko?"

"Why, in my arms, of course," said Mrs. Monkey. "How else would any sensible animal carry anything?" And she whisked away through the trees.

"Oh dear," said Katy, and a great big tear ran across her long nose. "I can't carry anything in these short little arms, oh *dear!* She wasn't any help at all. What are we going to do?" And she just sat down and cried harder than ever.

Poor Freddy! He hated to see his mother cry, so he put his paw to his head and he thought, and thought, and *thought*.

"What about the lion?" he asked
when Katy stopped crying a little.

"They don't carry their children. The poor
things walk just the way you do," said
Katy.

"There's — there's birds," said Freddy.
"How do they carry their babies?"

"Birds!" said Katy. "The mother birds
push their children out of the nest and they
squawk and shriek and flap their wings
about it."

Then all at once Katy Kangaroo stopped
crying and looked at Freddy. "They do say
that the owl knows almost everything," she
said slowly.

"Well, then, for goodness' sake, let's ask *him!*" said Freddy. They found the owl asleep in an old dead tree, and he was cross because he didn't want to be waked up in the middle of the day. But when he saw that Katy was so sad he came out, blinking and ruffling his feathers and said in a scratchy voice, "Well! Well! what is it? Speak up! And speak loudly. I'm deaf as a post."

So Katy stood under the tree and screamed at him, "I'm a mother kangaroo and I haven't a pocket to carry my child in. How shall I carry him? What shall I do?"

"Get a pocket," said the owl and went to sleep again.

"Where?" cried Katy. "Oh, please, don't go to sleep before you tell me where!"

"How should I know?" said the owl. "They sell that sort of thing in the City, I believe. Now, kindly go away and let me sleep."

"The City!" said Katy, and looked at Freddy with big, round eyes. "Of course, we'll go to the City!"

Katy was so excited that she almost left
Freddy behind as she went leaping over
bushes and hopping along the path, singing
in a sort of hummy way a little song she
had just made up:

   "Hippity! Hoppity!
   Flippity! Floppity!
   Wasn't it a pity?
   I didn't know
   It was to the City
   I should go!"

She hopped so fast that Freddy could hardly keep up, but at last they left the woods behind and came to the City where there were stores and houses and automobiles.

The people all stared and stared at Katy, but she didn't notice it. She was looking for pockets and she saw that almost everybody had them.

And then, all at once, she saw — she could hardly believe it — a man who seemed to be ALL pockets!

He was simply covered with pockets. Big pockets, little pockets, medium-sized pockets —

Katy went up to him and laid a paw on his arm. He was a little frightened, but Katy looked at him with her soft brown eyes and said, "Please, dear, kind man, where did you get all those pockets?"

"These pockets?" he said. "You want to know where I got all these pockets? Why, they just came with the apron, of course."

"You mean you can really get something to put on with ALL those pockets already in it?" asked Katy.

"Sure you can," said the man. "I keep my hammer and nails and tools in my pockets, but I can get another apron, so I'll give you mine."

He took off the apron and dumped it UPSIDE DOWN.

Out fell a saw, wrench, nails, a hammer, a drill, and lots of other tools.

Then the man shook the apron hard and turned it right side up again and hung it around Katy's neck and tied it behind her back.

Katy was so pleased and excited and happy that she couldn't speak. She just stood still and looked down at the pockets and smiled and smiled and smiled.

By this time, a big crowd had gathered to see what Katy Kangaroo was doing. When they saw how pleased she was, they all smiled, too.

At last Katy was able to say "Thank you" to the nice, kind man, and then what do you think she did? She popped Freddy into a very comfortable pocket and she hippity-hopped home faster than ever before because, of course, she didn't have to wait for Freddy.

And when she got home, what do you think she did?

Well, she had so many pockets that she put Freddy into the biggest one of all. Then, into the next largest she put little Leonard Lion. Thomas Tortoise just fitted into another pocket.

Sometimes she had a baby bird if its mother was busy at a worm hunt. And there was still room for a monkey, a skunk, a rabbit, a raccoon, a lizard, a squirrel, a 'possum, a turtle, a frog, and a snail.

So now, all the animals like Katy's pockets better than any other pockets in the whole forest.

And Katy Kangaroo is very happy
because now
SHE HAS MORE POCKETS THAN
ANY MOTHER KANGAROO
IN THE WORLD!

Pockets

by Mary Ann Hoberman

Pockets hold things
Pockets hide things
Special private dark inside things.
Pockets save things
Pockets keep things
Secret silent way down deep things.

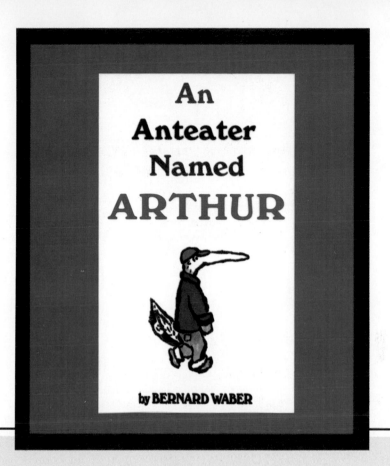

An
Anteater
Named
ARHTUR

by BERNARD WABER

Gregory was not a good eater and Katy had no pocket. Nobody's perfect, not even Arthur the anteater. He may remind you of someone you know.

Bernard Waber wrote *An Anteater Named Arthur* and he drew the pictures.

5

Once Upon a Time

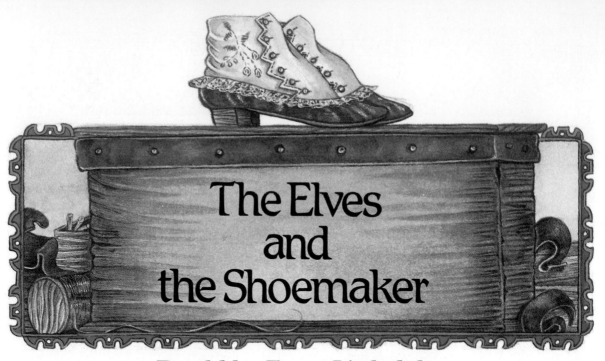

The Elves
and
the Shoemaker

Retold by Freya Littledale
Illustrated by Pat and Robin DeWitt

There was once a good shoemaker who became very poor.

At last he had only one piece of leather to make one pair of shoes.

"Well," said the shoemaker to his wife, "I will cut the leather tonight and make the shoes in the morning."

The next morning he went to his table, and he couldn't believe what he saw.

The leather was polished. The sewing
was done. And there was a fine pair of
shoes! Not one stitch was out of place.

"Do you see what I see?" asked the
shoemaker.

"Indeed I do," said his wife. "I see a fine
pair of shoes."

"But who could have made them?" the
shoemaker said.

"It's just like magic!" said his wife.

At that very moment a man came in
with a top hat and cane.

"Those shoes look right for me," said the
man.

And so they were. They were right from heel to toe.

"How much do they cost?"

"One gold coin," said the shoemaker.

"I'll give you two," said the man.

And he went on his way with a smile on his face and the new shoes on his feet.

"Well, well," said the shoemaker, "now I can buy leather for two pairs of shoes." And he cut the leather that night so he could make the shoes in the morning.

The next morning the shoemaker woke up, and he found two pairs of ladies' shoes. They were shining in the sunlight.

"Who is making these shoes?" said the shoemaker. "They are the best shoes in the world."

At that very moment two ladies came in. They looked exactly alike.

"My, what pretty shoes!" said the ladies. "They will surely fit us."

And the ladies were right.

They gave the shoemaker four gold coins and away they went . . . clickety-clack, clickety-clack in their pretty new shoes.

And so it went.

Every night the shoemaker cut the leather. Every morning the shoes were made. And every day more people came to buy his beautiful shoes.

Just before Christmas the shoemaker said, "Whoever is making these shoes is making us very happy."

"And rich," said his wife.

"Let us stay up and see who it is," the shoemaker said.

"Good," said his wife. So they hid behind some coats, and they waited and waited and waited.

When the clock struck twelve, in came two little elves. *"Elves,"* cried the shoemaker.

"Shh!" said his wife.

At once the elves hopped up on the table and set to work.

Tap-tap went their hammers. Snip-snap went their scissors. Stitch-stitch went their needles.

Their tiny fingers moved so fast the shoemaker and his wife could hardly believe their eyes.

The elves sewed and they hammered and they didn't stop until all the shoes were finished. There were little shoes and big ones. There were white ones and black ones and brown ones.

The elves lined them all in a row. Then they jumped down from the table. They ran across the room and out the door.

The next morning the wife said, "The elves have made us very happy. I want to make them happy too. They need new clothes to keep warm.

So I'll make them pants and shirts and coats. And I'll knit them socks and hats. You can make them each a pair of shoes."

"Yes, yes!" said the shoemaker. And they went right to work.

On Christmas Eve the shoemaker left no leather on the table. He left all the pretty gifts instead.

Then he and his wife hid behind the coats to see what the elves would do.

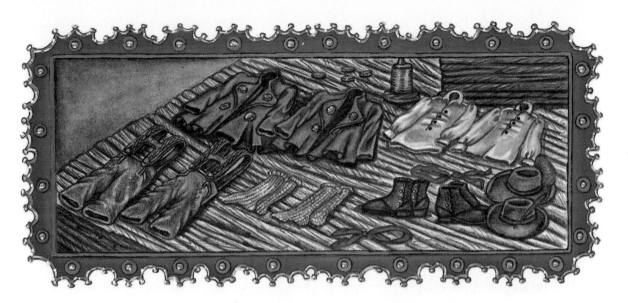

When the clock struck twelve, in came
the elves, ready to set to work.

But when they looked at the table and
saw the fine clothes, they laughed and
clapped their hands.

"How happy they are!" said the
shoemaker's wife.

"Shhh," said her husband.

The elves put on the clothes, looked in
the mirror, and began to sing:

> *What fine and handsome elves are we,*
> *No longer cobblers will we be.*
> *From now on we'll dance and play,*
> *Into the woods and far away.*

They hopped over the table and jumped over the chairs.

They skipped all around the room, danced out the door, and were never seen again.

But from that night on everything always went well for the good shoemaker and his wife.

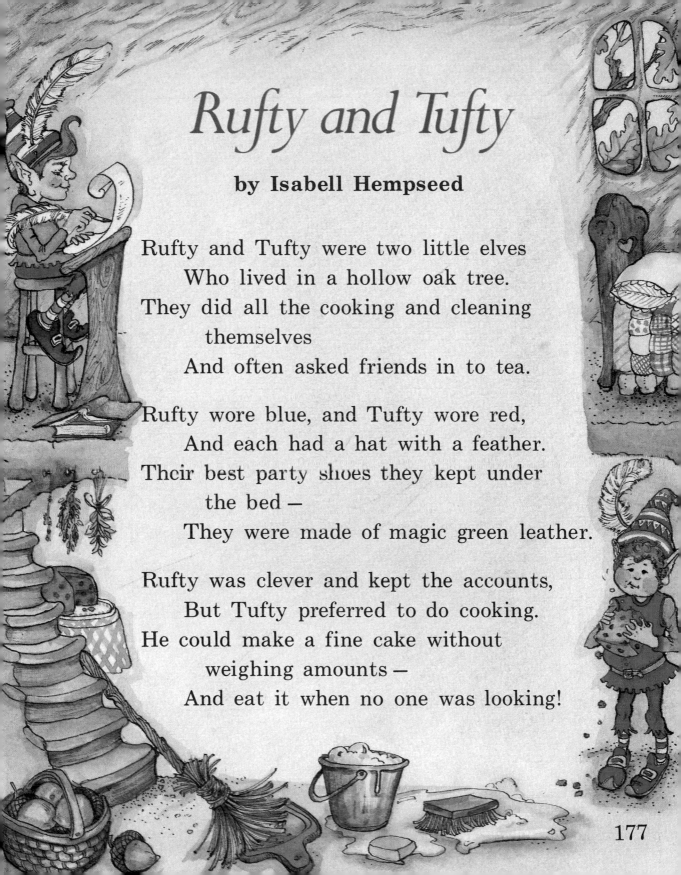

Rufty and Tufty

by Isabell Hempseed

Rufty and Tufty were two little elves
    Who lived in a hollow oak tree.
They did all the cooking and cleaning
      themselves
    And often asked friends in to tea.

Rufty wore blue, and Tufty wore red,
    And each had a hat with a feather.
Their best party shoes they kept under
      the bed —
    They were made of magic green leather.

Rufty was clever and kept the accounts,
    But Tufty preferred to do cooking.
He could make a fine cake without
      weighing amounts —
    And eat it when no one was looking!

THE GIANT
WHO THREW
TANTRUMS

A story from *The Book of Giant Stories*

by David L. Harrison
Illustrated by Philippe Fix

At the foot of Mount Thistle lay a
village. In the village lived a little boy who
liked to go walking.

One Saturday afternoon the little boy
was walking in the woods when he was
startled by a terrible noise. He popped
behind a bush.

Before long a huge giant came stamping
down the path. He looked upset.

"Tanglebangled ringlepox!" the giant
bellowed. He banged his head against a tree
until the leaves shook off like snowflakes.

"Franglewhangled whippersnack!" the giant roared. Yanking up the tree, he whirled it around his head and knocked down twenty-seven other trees.

Muttering to himself, he stalked up the path toward the top of Mount Thistle.

The little boy hurried home.

"I just saw a giant throwing a tantrum!" he told everyone in the village. They only smiled.

"There's no such thing as a giant," the mayor assured him.

"He knocked down twenty-seven trees," said the little boy.

"Must have been a tornado," the weatherman said with a nod. "Happens around here all the time."

The next Saturday afternoon the little boy again went walking. Before long he heard a horrible noise. He zipped behind a tree.

Soon the same giant came storming down the path. He still looked upset.

"Pollywogging frizzlesnatch!" he hollered. Throwing himself down, he pounded the ground with both fists.

Boulders bounced like popcorn.

Scowling crossly, the giant puckered his lips into an "O." He drew in his breath sharply. It sounded like somebody slurping soup.

"Pooh!" he cried.

Grabbing his left foot with both hands, the giant hopped on his right foot up the path toward the top of Mount Thistle.

The little boy hurried home.

"That giant's at it again," he told everyone. "He threw such a tantrum that the ground trembled!"

"Must have been an earthquake," the police chief said. "Happens around here sometimes."

The next Saturday afternoon the little boy again went walking. Before long he heard a frightening noise. He plopped behind a rock.

Soon the giant came fuming down the path. When he reached the little boy's rock, he puckered his lips into an "O."

He drew in his breath sharply with a loud, soup-slurping sound. "Phooey!" he cried. "I *never* get it right!"

The giant held his breath until his face turned blue and his eyes rolled up. "Fozzlehumper backawacket!" he panted. Then he lumbered up the path toward the top of Mount Thistle.

The little boy followed him. Up and up and up he climbed to the very top of Mount Thistle.

There he discovered a huge cave. A surprising sound was coming from it. The giant was crying!

"All I want is to whistle," he sighed through his tears. "But every time I try, it comes out wrong!"

The little boy had just learned to whistle. He knew how hard it could be. He stepped inside the cave.

The giant looked surprised. "How did *you* get here?"

"I know what you're doing wrong," the little boy said.

When the giant heard that, he leaned down and put his hands on his knees.

"Tell me at once!" he begged.

"You have to stop throwing tantrums," the little boy told him.

"I promise!" said the giant, who didn't want anyone thinking he had poor manners.

"Pucker your lips . . ." the little boy said.

"I always do!" the giant assured him.

"Then blow," the little boy added.

"Blow?"

"Blow."

The giant looked as if he didn't believe it. He puckered his lips into an "O." He blew. Out came a long, low whistle. It sounded like a train locomotive. The giant smiled.

He shouted, "I whistled! Did you hear that? I whistled!"

Taking the little boy's hand, he danced
in a circle.

"You're a good friend," the giant said.

"Thank you," said the little boy. "Sometime maybe we can whistle together. But right now I have to go. It's my suppertime."

The giant stood before his cave and waved good-by.

The little boy seldom saw the giant after that. But the giant kept his promise about not throwing tantrums.

"We never have earthquakes," the mayor liked to say.

"Haven't had a tornado in ages," the weatherman would add.

Now and then they heard a long, low whistle somewhere in the distance.

"Must be a train," the police chief would say.

But the little boy knew his friend the giant was walking up the path toward the top of Mount Thistle — whistling.

Once upon a time elves made shoes, and a giant learned to whistle! What next?

It's *Rumpelstiltskin* — a very old story retold by Paul O. Zelinsky. Find out what happens when a girl has to spin straw into gold.

6

Friends

BIRTHDAYS

Excerpts from *Little Owl, Keeper of the Trees*

by Ronald and Ann Himler

Illustrated by Ronald Himler

Little Owl rolled over in his bed and tucked
the covers up around him. He listened to the
rainfall on the leaves outside. He liked the
sound of rain. He liked it so much he fell
asleep.

When he woke up, the rain had stopped.

Moonlight came through the bedroom
window.

Suddenly, Little Owl sat up.

"Tonight is my birthday!" he cried aloud. He threw back the covers and ran into the kitchen.

"Good evening, Little Owl." His mother smiled. "Are you ready for breakfast?"

"I'm hungry," said Little Owl, sitting down at the table. "Do you know what tonight is?"

"Yes, I do," said Mrs. Owl, as she put two big slices of toast with black-currant jam before him. "Tonight is the night I must clean the cupboards."

"No, no!" said Little Owl. "I mean, do you know what *tonight* is? It's special."

"There's nothing special about cleaning cupboards," said Mother, laughing. She poured Little Owl a glass of milk and went back to her work.

After breakfast. Little Owl went outside. "She forgot," he said to himself, going down the steps of the old Sycamore Tree.

"She forgot that tonight is my birthday. This never happened before." Little Owl sighed.

A cool breeze was scattering the last of the rain clouds. Stars twinkled in the patches of clear sky.

Little Owl walked slowly out into the wild fields. The high, wet grass glistened like silver in the moonlight. Little Owl brushed back the wet grass with his wing and the grass sprang back, showering him with raindrops. It tickled, and this made him laugh.

As he came to the tall oaks at the edge of the field, he saw Raccoon sitting beneath a tree.

"Hi, Raccoon," said Little Owl. "Do you know what tonight is?"

"You bet I do," said Raccoon.

"You do?" cried Little Owl.

"Tonight's the night my cousin promised to show me his secret fishing place."

"Oh," said Little Owl. "I thought you *knew*."

"I've been waiting here since sunset," Raccoon went on. "but he hasn't come yet. Well, I can't wait any longer. I'm going down to the old rock by the river and fish."

"Can I come?" asked Little Owl.

"Listen, Little Owl," said Raccoon. "You know what you can do? When my cousin comes by, tell him I'm down at the river. Will you do that, Little Owl?"

Then Raccoon hurried off without waiting for an answer.

Little Owl was left alone in the
moonlight. He stood for a while, looking
down the path. But no one came.

I'm not going to stand here all night, he
thought. Not on my birthday.

Little Owl wrote a note for Raccoon's
cousin and stuck it on the tree. Then he
stepped back and looked at the note.

Suppose, he thought, suppose that note was a sign that said. "Tonight is Little Owl's birthday." And there were signs just like it all over the forest. Then everyone would know about my birthday.

"Everyone!" he cried aloud. "That's it — I'll make signs."

Little Owl ran back through the wild fields, with his wings out, making the raindrops fly. He laughed all the way across the fields.

He went into the cellar of the old Sycamore Tree. There, among all the dusty chests, boxes, picture frames, and cans of paint, he found a stack of boards.

Little Owl spread all the boards out in the middle of the floor. Then he opened a can of blue paint. He dipped the tip of one feather into the paint and wrote on the first board: "Tonight is Little Owl's birthday."

I'll put this sign down by the river, Little Owl thought. He painted some water at the bottom of the sign to remember where it should go.

Then he dipped another feather into a can of green paint. "I'll put this sign on the old tree in the hollow," he said. So he painted some leaves at the bottom of the sign.

Next, Little Owl dipped another feather into the red paint. "I'll put this one on the bridge," he said. And he carefully drew a picture of the old bridge at the bottom of the sign.

He dipped another feather into the yellow paint. "I'll put this one by the wild fields." Little Owl painted tall grass all around the edge of the sign.

201

Then he started all over again, first with the blue, then the green, then the red, and last the yellow. He went on in this way until all the boards were painted. On each sign he painted a mark, so he would remember where to put it.

When he was done, Little Owl looked at his wing. Each feather was a different color. He liked it so much, he dipped his other wing in the colors, too.

"Now I even look like a birthday owl." He laughed.

Little Owl picked up all the signs and carried them off down the path.

"Here's the guardian of the forest, the keeper of the trees, bringing an important message to all the creatures in the forest," Little Owl said to himself.

The path led away from the river into the deep woods. At the edge of the hollow was a great maple tree that had been split by lightning.

Into the crack of the tree, Little Owl
wedged the green sign.

He stepped back to see how it looked. It
fell down.

"Phooey!" said Little Owl. He picked up
the sign and wedged it in again.

Again it fell out.

"I'll just have to go back and get a
hammer and nail it up," said Little Owl.

He left the pile of signs near the bottom
of the tree and went home.

When he came back, all the signs were gone. Someone was hammering furiously down in the hollow. Little Owl left the path and went down into the low hollow.

It was a damp, lonely place, overgrown with clumps of sedge grass and brambles. The trees were old, and their roots twisted and stuck out above the ground. The cool night breeze had scattered the mists which usually hung over the hollow.

Suddenly, the hammering stopped. Mole poked his head around the stump of a tree.

"Is that you, Little Owl?" he said in a slow, sad voice. "It's me — Mole."

"Hello, Mole," said Little Owl. "I haven't seen you in a long time."

"No one usually does," said Mole. He came around and sat on a gnarled root in front of Little Owl. "But I saw you, Little Owl," he said shyly. "Yes I did."

Mole sat with his head down, staring at his toes. "Oh, Little Owl, you have made me very happy," he said.

"I have?" asked Little Owl. "You don't look happy."

"Oh, I always look like this." sighed Mole. "But tonight, I *am* happy. Do you know what tonight is, Little Owl?"

"I do!" said Little Owl excitedly. "Do you know?"

"Tonight is my birthday," said Mole, proudly.

"*Your* birthday!" gasped Little Owl.

"Every year tonight is my birthday," Mole went on, "but no one ever knows. I don't suppose it really matters much, though it does make a difference somehow. But you remembered, Little Owl."

"I did?" asked Little Owl.

"Yes, you did," Mole continued. "You said to yourself, 'Tonight must be Mole's birthday and I'm going to make him a wonderful present.' So you made that present, Little Owl. You brought it here and set it down near my hole. Then you hurried off so that I would be surprised."

"But I saw you, Little Owl. I was just poking around here, all by myself, as usual, when I saw you do it."

"Oh, Little Owl," said Mole, getting up slowly, "I'm so happy! Come and see."

Mole led Little Owl down to a corner of the hollow. "Look!" he said proudly.

"My signs!" cried Little Owl.

"My new house," sighed Mole. "Isn't it beautiful?"

Little Owl could hardly believe his eyes. Mole was building a house out of Little Owl's signs.

"I've always wanted a real house," said Mole. "And now, because of your wonderful present, I shall have one. I'll sit in it all day long and look at the lovely decorations you painted for me."

Mole could not read. In fact, he could not even see very well.

"Oh, it will be a happy home," said Mole. "And a happy birthday."

Little Owl looked at his signs.

Some of them were already nailed together. "Now no one will ever know," he sighed to himself.

Then Little Owl looked at Mole's happy face. He picked up his hammer and helped Mole build his house.

He nailed the blue board to the red, red to the yellow, green toward the door. That's the way Mole liked it.

When they were finished, they sat together on a small stump and admired the house.

"Do you know what tonight is, Mole? Tonight is my birthday, too," said Little Owl, beaming.

"Your birthday and my birthday on the same night?" cried Mole.

"That's right," said Little Owl. "Let's go to my house and celebrate our birthdays together."

Mole was delighted. He had never celebrated anything with anyone before.

Little Owl and Mole came out of the hollow and together they started down the path. The deep night sky was filled with stars. Fireflies blinked at them from the shadows of the wood. Crickets sang under the leaves. On the way home, Little Owl taught Mole a birthday song.

They climbed the steps of the old Sycamore Tree. A glow of colored lights came from the kitchen window.

Little Owl opened the door.

"Surprise!" everyone shouted. "Happy birthday, Little Owl!"

Little Owl couldn't believe his eyes. The kitchen was all decorated with lights and colored paper. The table was set for a party.

Around it stood Raccoon and his cousin, Old Possum and his nephew, the gray rabbit and his sister, and all Little Owl's friends.

Mole was so startled, he hid behind Little Owl. "What's going on?" he asked timidly.

"It's a birthday party!" cried Little Owl.

He ran over to his mother and gave her a big hug. "You remembered after all!"

"Remembered what?" his mother laughed.

"You remembered my birthday. And it's Mole's birthday, too," said Little Owl.

Mole was still standing back in the doorway. Little Owl brought him right into the middle of the party.

"Happy birthday, Mole," said Mrs. Owl.

"Happy birthday, Mole. Happy birthday, Little Owl!" everyone cried in one voice.

Then Mrs. Owl brought out a big cake with HAPPY BIRTHDAY spelled out in black currants.

Everyone ate and laughed together. Then they all sang songs. Mole sang the birthday song Little Owl had taught him.

Nannabah's Friend

From the book by Mary Perrine

Illustrated by Margaret Sanfilippo

Big Star was still shining through the round hole-for-smoke of their hogan roof when Nannabah's grandmother shook her very gently to wake her.

"Get up quickly, my grandchild," she said.

Nannabah sat up on her bed made from sheepskin and stretched until the sleep was out of her eyes.

Her grandmother was taking down from the hogan wall the pan for cooking their breakfast of bread-you-slap-with-your-hands. Nannabah could smell the piñon fire made outside by her grandfather.

Nannabah went outside and sat by her grandfather on his bright colored blanket. Nannabah and her grandfather sat close together in quietness.

Nannabah could hear her grandmother slapping dough in their hogan. Nannabah wanted to run to her and ask her, "My grandmother, is it today I must take your sheep to the canyon alone?" And she wanted to say, "I think you told my grandfather." But she was afraid to hear her grandmother's answer, so she stayed by the piñon fire with her grandfather.

Later Nannabah's grandmother was kneeling by the fire cooking round thin pieces of dough. Nannabah tried to see her eyes, but her grandmother didn't look at her until after they began to eat.

Then her grandmother looked at her with gentleness, and Nannabah knew she was going to say it. "Today, my grandchild, I won't go with you when you take the sheep."

Nannabah wanted to hide her face with her hands, and she tried. But her grandmother and grandfather must have seen through her fingers.

"Don't cry, grandchild," her grandmother said. And her grandfather put his hand on her shoulder with kindness.

When it was time to take the sheep to the canyon, Nannabah's grandmother opened the gate for the sheep. She handed Nannabah a stick to drive them, and a can with little rocks in it.

Nannabah hit the sheep very gently with her grandmother's stick and started them up the trail. She kept looking back on her way up the mesa. From the top of the mesa she could see her grandmother piling wood by their hogan door.

After a while Nannabah started the sheep down the trail on the other side of the mesa. For a long time the sheep walked slowly on the trail.

Then a big sheep with horns left the trail and the others began to follow. Nannabah ran after the big sheep with horns and tried to stop it, but the big sheep with horns went around her.

Soon it started up the hill and the others followed. Nannabah went in front of them and tried to push them with her foot, but she wasn't strong enough.

Then she thought of the can with little rocks in it. She took the can and shook it.

As if they had heard a snake, the sheep stopped moving. Then, slowly, they turned and walked away from Nannabah, and soon they were going down the trail again.

When they had almost come to the canyon's flat ground, the big sheep with horns started from the trail again. Two others began to follow. But Nannabah went ahead of them, and shook the can with little rocks in it, and the sheep went back.

Finally they were in the canyon. There was a place near the canyon's end where water fell from rocks and made a pool below.

Around the water, the grass was green. The sheep stopped there, and began to graze, and Nannabah sat down by them in the grass.

For a long time she watched the water that was running down the rocks and she listened to its sound. Then she looked up at the sky and clouds.

She thought about her grandmother and grandfather. And she thought about her mother and father, and her little sister and baby brother who were in their hogan that was far away. She was going to hide her eyes with her hands and cry, but she had never cried alone before. She had never been alone before.

Nannabah stood up and began to walk among the sheep by the water. Red mud was by the edge of the water, and Nannabah touched the mud with her fingers to feel its softness. Then, an idea came to her.

She filled her hand with red mud. Using a stick to help her fingers shape the mud, she made a doll. She named it "Little Sister."

Then she got more mud and made another doll. This doll was a baby in a cradleboard and Nannabah named it "Baby Brother."

She put Little Sister and Baby Brother on a flat rock in the sun to dry. She thought of the sheep then, and she watched them for a while. All of them were grazing in the deep grass by the water, and they were all near.

Nannabah began to make a hogan for Little Sister and Baby Brother. For the wall, she rolled red mud in her hands to make logs. She curved the logs of mud until they were round like bracelets. The roof was made from a thin piece of mud. Before she put the roof on, she made a round hole-for-smoke.

When the hogan was finished, she put Little Sister and Baby Brother on the floor inside. "It is a nice home," thought Nannabah. Then she took Little Sister and Baby Brother from the little hogan and put them on the ground outside. Nannabah was going to talk to them, but she remembered that they had no ears. And she remembered, suddenly, that she was still alone.

She looked up at Sun. Her grandmother had told her once that when it was time to start the sheep from the canyon Sun would be standing over the tallest rock. Soon Sun was there.

Nannabah put Little Sister and Baby Brother inside the little hogan. She was glad she had made them, and she was glad she had made them a home. But still she wished she could talk with them.

Then she hit the sheep gently with her grandmother's stick, and soon they were on the trail.

It wasn't long until they had come to the top of the mesa.

From the mesa, Nannabah could see her grandmother and grandfather near the hogan. Her grandmother was weaving a rug on her loom by the door. Her grandfather was carrying corn from the wagon.

When Nannabah had come home with the sheep, her grandmother opened the gate again and helped her drive the sheep inside.

The next morning, when her grandmother shook her to wake her, Big Star was looking again through the round hole-for-smoke. Nannabah thought first about Little Sister and Baby Brother in the little hogan. Big Star, she thought, must be looking at them too. There was no one to wake them.

When her grandmother had made their bread-you-slap-with-your-hands, Nannabah ate with her grandmother and grandfather. Then she went to the corral. Nannabah's grandmother opened the gate for the sheep, and Nannabah started them up to the mesa.

On the other side of the mesa, tall rocks hid the canyon's floor. Nannabah looked between some of them trying to see the little hogan, but other tall rocks stood behind. Then, near the end of the trail, one rock was low. Nannabah ran ahead of the sheep and climbed up on it.

She could see the little hogan — and something else. Sheep were grazing in the grass by the water, and a girl was sitting near the little hogan — a real girl.

Nannabah wanted to run ahead of her sheep again, but she was afraid. She wondered if the girl would smile and talk to her and listen when she talked.

When Nannabah's sheep came to the green grass, Nannabah and the other girl looked at each other with shyness.

Nannabah sat down and took Little Sister and Baby Brother from their little hogan. She put Baby Brother in her lap, and she handed Little Sister to the other girl to hold in her lap.

The girl smiled then, and talked. "When I saw the dolls and the little hogan," she said, "I wished the person who made them would come back and be my friend."

Then Nannabah smiled and said, "I think I made little Sister and Baby Brother because I wished that you would come and be my friend."

When Sun stood over the tallest rock Nannabah and the other girl went different ways from the canyon with their sheep.

Every morning after that, when Nannabah ran ahead of her sheep and climbed onto the low rock, she saw her friend waiting by the little hogan.

227

Little Puppy

From the Navajo

by Hilda Faunce Wetherill

Little puppy with the black spots,
Come and herd the flock with me.
We will climb the red rocks
And from the top we'll see
The tall cliffs, the straight cliffs,
The fluted cliffs,
Where the eagles live.

We'll see the dark rocks,
The smooth rocks,
That hold the rain to give us
Water, when we eat our bread and meat,
When the sun is high.
Little spotted dog of mine,
Come and spend the day with me.
When the sun is going down
Behind the pointed hill,
We will follow home the flock.
They will lead the way
To the hogans where the fires burn
And the square cornbread is in the ashes,
Waiting our return.

SAY HELLO, VANESSA

by Marjorie Weinman Sharmat

Illustrated by Alan Baker

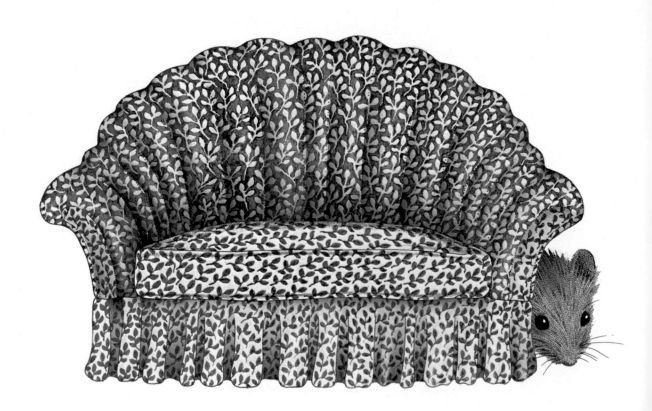

Vanessa Mouse lived with her mother and father on three floors of a fine, old house.

Mrs. Mouse had many friends. When they came to visit, Vanessa hid under the sofa and peeked out.

"Say hello, Vanessa," said her mother.

But Vanessa didn't.

When Mr. Mouse's friends came over, Vanessa sat in a corner and didn't look up.

"Look up, Vanessa," said her father.

But Vanessa wouldn't.

No friends came over to see Vanessa.
Because Vanessa didn't have any.

"Not one friend," said Mrs. Mouse sadly.
"Not even a now-and-then friend. Or an
every Sunday friend. Or a rainy day,
sit-by-the-window-and-nibble-crumbs friend.
Nobody."

"Trying to make friends must be the
scariest thing in the world," said Vanessa.

"Well, the first time might be a little
scary," said Mrs. Mouse. "But why don't you
try it?"

The next day Vanessa went to school. She took her seat in class behind Quincy Moose. "It's wonderful hiding here behind Quincy Moose's antlers," thought Vanessa.

Mr. Mitchell, the teacher, said, "Today we'll start with spelling."

He looked at Andrew Aardvark. "Andrew, how do you spell country?"

"Does it begin with a *k*?" asked Andrew.

"No, I'm afraid it doesn't," said Mr. Mitchell. He looked at Craig Badger. "Can you spell country, Craig?"

"Does it end with an *e*?" asked Craig.

"No," said Mr. Mitchell, "it doesn't. Who knows how to spell country?"

Vanessa started to raise her hand. "I know how, I know how," she said to herself. Then she lowered her hand. "But I can't. Everybody will look at me and my funny teeth and my furry face. Maybe I'll spell country tomorrow."

After class, everyone got together in little bunches and groups. Except Vanessa who was all alone.

"Bunches and groups, bunches and groups," thought Vanessa. "Everybody has enough friends already. They don't need me."

When she got home, her mother asked, "Well, Vanessa, did you make a friend today?"

"No," said Vanessa. And she told her mother about bunches and groups.

"I understand," said Mrs. Mouse. "But if you look hard enough, you'll find someone who is alone. Then you can go up and say hello."

"I'll try that," said Vanessa.

At school the next morning, Mr. Mitchell asked, "Who has learned to spell country?"

Everyone looked around.

"Here's a chance that might never come again," thought Vanessa.

Vanessa started to raise her hand. But she put it down again. "Maybe tomorrow I'll do it," she thought.

When class was over, Vanessa saw Lisa
Goat standing alone against a wall.

Slowly Vanessa went up to Lisa. Then
Vanessa whispered, "Hello."

"What?" asked Lisa.

"Hello," whispered Vanessa.

"What?" asked Lisa again.

Vanessa walked away.

She ran home to her mother. "I said hello
but I didn't make a friend," said Vanessa.

"Saying hello usually works," said Mrs. Mouse.

"It didn't for me," said Vanessa. "I went up to Lisa Goat very politely and said hello, just like that, but all she said was *what?*"

"Try again tomorrow with someone else," said Mrs. Mouse. "And speak a little louder."

"I'll try," said Vanessa.

Vanessa hurried to school the next morning and took her seat behind Quincy Moose.

Mr. Mitchell asked, "Who can spell country?"

"Me!" shouted Andrew Aardvark.

"I can, too," said Craig Badger.

"C-o-u-n-t-r-y!" someone else spelled.

"Nuts!" thought Vanessa. "Well, anyway, the day isn't over yet."

Vanessa walked up and down the hall looking for someone who was alone. At last she saw Sigmund Toad counting the pencils in his pencil pouch.

Vanessa walked up to him.

"HELLO!" she shouted.

Sigmund dropped
his pencil pouch.

"HELLO!" she shouted again.

Sigmund put his hands over his ears and
hopped away.

That night Vanessa told her mother about
her new hello.

"Maybe a medium hello will work," said
Mrs. Mouse.

"I don't want to try any more hellos," said
Vanessa.

The next day Vanessa's mind was made
up. "Today I will not say anything. Not
anything at all!" she said to herself.

She took her seat behind Quincy Moose.

"This morning we have a new word to
spell, and it's a difficult one," said Mr.
Mitchell. "Does anyone know how to spell
tooth?"

"Oh!" thought Vanessa. "I do! I know that word!"

Mr. Mitchell looked around.

Andrew was squirming in his seat. Craig was pulling on his ear.

Vanessa felt hot and thumpy inside. She was thinking, "Tooth is such a great word to know how to spell, and *I* know how to spell it!"

Suddenly Vanessa raised her hand high. And higher. She wiggled it. She waved it. She said, "*I* can spell tooth! I can spell it! T-o-o-t-h!"

"Perfect," said Mr. Mitchell.

Everyone was looking at Vanessa. But she didn't mind. In fact she felt good.

After class was over, Vanessa gathered up her books.

Suddenly Quincy Moose turned around. "I wish I knew how to spell tooth," he said. "I wish I knew how to spell moose."

"Moose is easy," said Vanessa. "It's like mouse except it has an *o* where the *u* is."

Vanessa and Quincy walked out of class together.

They sat on a bench and talked about *mouse* and *moose*.

"That was fun," said Quincy. "Let's do it again."

"Want to come to my house?" asked Vanessa.

"Sure," said Quincy.

Vanessa and Quincy walked
to Vanessa's house.

They passed Mr. Mitchell.

"Hello, Mr. Mitchell," said Vanessa.

They passed Andrew Aardvark.

"Hi there, Andrew," said Vanessa.

They passed Craig Badger.

"How are you, Craig?" said Vanessa.

They passed Lisa Goat.

"Greetings, Lisa," said Vanessa.

They passed Sigmund Toad.

"Nice day, Sigmund!" said Vanessa.

When Vanessa got home, she ran into the house.

"Mother! Mother! I brought someone home!"

"I'm Quincy Moose. M-o-o-s-e," said Quincy. "And you must be Mrs. Mouse. M-o-u-s-e."

"And you must be Vanessa's friend," said Mrs. Mouse.

"That's who I am!" said Quincy.

"A friend is fun to have," said Vanessa. "Especially an everyday, sit-by-the-fire-and-talk friend."

You've read several stories about making new friends. Now read about Bidemmi who likes to draw pictures and tell stories to her friend. You'll find out how *Cherries and Cherry Pits*, by Vera B. Williams, got its name.

Sharing

The Rabbit and the Turnip

Translated by Richard Sadler
Illustrated by Carol Leeson

One wintry day, when snow lay deep on the ground, Little Rabbit went out to look for food and he found two turnips. He gobbled up one of them. Then he said: "It is snowing so hard and it is so bitterly cold that perhaps Little Donkey has nothing to eat. I shall take him my other turnip."

Off he ran to Little Donkey's house. But Little Donkey was out, so Little Rabbit left the turnip on Little Donkey's doorstep and hopped back home.

Now Little Donkey had also gone out to look for food and he found some potatoes.

When he got home and saw the turnip
he was most surprised. Who could have put
it there? Then he said to himself: It is
snowing so hard and it is so bitterly cold,
perhaps Little Sheep has nothing to eat. I
shall take it to her.

At once he rolled the turnip to Little Sheep's house. But there was no sign of Little Sheep, so he left the turnip on Little Sheep's table and cantered back home.

Meanwhile, Little Sheep, who had also been looking for food, had found a cabbage and was happily trotting home to eat it.

When she got to her house and found the turnip she was astonished. Who could have put it there? Little Sheep decided to give the turnip to Little Doe. It was snowing so hard and it was so bitterly cold, she felt sure Little Doe would be feeling hungry.

So Little Sheep took the turnip to Little Doe's house. But there was no one at home, so she left the turnip on Little Doe's window sill and off she went.

It so happened that Little Doe was also out looking for food and *she* found some fresh green leaves.

She, too, was very surprised to find the turnip waiting for her at home. "I shall give this beautiful turnip to Little Rabbit," she said to herself. "It is snowing so hard and it is so bitterly cold that perhaps he has nothing to eat."

At once Little Doe ran to Little Rabbit's house. And there was Little Rabbit, fast asleep. Little Doe did not want to wake him up, so she nudged the turnip gently inside the doorway and hurried away.

When Little Rabbit woke up and found
the turnip, he thought he must be
dreaming. He rubbed his eyes. Then he said
to himself: "How kind of someone to give
me this turnip!" and he gobbled it all up.

Sound of Water   by Mary O'Neill

The sound of water is:
Rain,
Lap,
Fold,
Slap,
Gurgle,
Splash,
Churn,
Crash,
Murmur,
Pour,
Ripple,
Roar,
Plunge,
Drip,
Spout,
Slip,
Sprinkle,
Flow,
Ice,
Snow.

255

A Special Trade

by **Sally Wittman**

Illustrated by Karen Gundersheimer

Old Bartholomew is Nelly's neighbor.

When Nelly was very small, he would take her every day for a walk down the block to Mrs. Pringle's vegetable garden. Bartholomew never pushed too fast. He always warned Nelly about Mr. Oliver's bumpy driveway:

"Hang on, Nell! Here's a bump!"

And she'd shout "BUMP!" as she rode over it.

If they met a nice dog along the way, they'd stop and pet it. But if it was nasty, Bartholomew would shoo it away.

When Mrs. Pringle's sprinkler was on, he would say, "Get ready, get set, CHAAARRRRRRRRRRRRRGE!"

Nelly would squeal "Wheeeee!" as he pushed her through it.

When Nelly began to walk, Bartholomew took her by the hand. "NO-NO!" she cried, pulling it back. Nelly didn't want any help.

So Bartholomew offered his hand only when she really needed it.

Bartholomew was
getting older, too. He
needed a walking stick.
So they walked very
slowly. When they
walked upstairs, they
both held on to the
railing.

The neighbors
called them "ham and
eggs" because they
were always together.
Even on Halloween. And on the
coldest day of winter when everyone
else was inside.

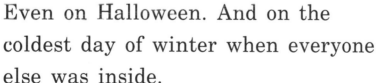

One summer Bartholomew taught Nelly
to skate by circling his walking stick. "Easy
does it!" he warned.

Then she skated right over his toes! He
wasn't mad, though. He just whistled and
rubbed his foot.

The first time Nelly tried to skate by
herself she fell. Bartholomew saw that she
felt like crying. He pulled up something
from the garden and said, "Don't be saddish,
have a radish!" Nelly laughed and ate it.
She didn't really like radishes, but she did
like Bartholomew.

Before long, Nelly was in school and Bartholomew had gotten even older. Sometimes he needed a helping hand, but he didn't like to take one. So Nelly held out her hand only when Bartholomew really needed it.

Whenever Bartholomew had to stop and rest, Nelly would beg for a story about the "old days."

Once after a story, she asked him, "Will we ever run out of things to talk about?"

"If we do," said Bartholomew, "we just won't say anything. Good friends can do that."

Some days they just took it easy and sat on the porch. Bartholomew would play a tune on his harmonica. Nelly would make up the words.

One day Bartholomew went out alone and fell down the stairs. An ambulance with a red flasher and a siren took him to the hospital.

He was gone for a long time.

Nelly wrote him every day. She always ended with, "Come back soon, so we can go for walks again."

When Bartholomew came home, he was in a wheelchair. The smile was gone from his eyes.

"I guess our walks
are over," he said.

"No they aren't,"
said Nelly. "*I* can take
you for walks now."

She knew just how
to do it, too. Nice and
easy, not too fast.

Just before Mr.
Oliver's driveway, she
would call, "Get ready
for the bump!"

And Bartholomew
would wave his hat
like a cowboy.

If they saw a nice dog,
they'd stop and pet it.
But if it was mean,
Nelly would shoo
it away.

One day when the sprinkler was on,
Nelly started to go around. But she changed
her mind. "All right, Bartholomew. Ready,
set, one, two, three."

"CHAAARRRRRRRRRRRRGE!" And
she pushed him right through it!

"Ah . . . that was fun!" said Bartholomew.
Nelly grinned. "I hope your wheelchair
won't rust."

"Fiddlesticks!" He laughed. "Who cares if
it does!"

Mrs. Pringle leaned over the fence. "Seems just like yesterday Bartholomew was pushing *you* in the stroller."

"That was when I was little," said Nelly. "Now it's my turn to push and Bartholomew's turn to sit . . . kind of like a trade."

Then they sat in the sun to dry. Nelly munched on a carrot. Bartholomew played a tune on his harmonica.

Nelly could see the old smile was back in Bartholomew's eyes.

ONE FINE DAY
by Nonny Hogrogian

Houghton Mifflin Literature

Sharing was important in the stories
you just read.

In *One Fine Day*, by Nonny Hogrogian, a
thirsty fox makes a big mistake. To make
things right again, he must find others
who are willing to share what they have.

8

Great Escapes

The Great Hamster Hunt

by Lenore Blegvad

Illustrated by Diet Van Beek

Nicholas wanted a hamster.

Mother said no to that.

"But Tony has a hamster," Nicholas said.

"Oh?" said Mother. "Then go next door and look at his."

"I don't think your mother likes little furry creatures," Father remarked.

"Well, Tony's mother doesn't either," Nicholas told him. "And *they* have one."

Mother sighed. "Then Tony's mother is just nicer than I am," she added. "Right?"

"I guess so," said Nicholas sadly.

One day Tony came to the door.

"We're going away for a week," he said to Nicholas's mother. "Do you think Nicholas would take care of my hamster for me if I asked him nicely?"

Nicholas jumped up from his chair.

"You don't have to ask me nicely," he shouted.

"The answer is *yes!*"

So Tony's hamster came to stay with
Nicholas for a week. Its name was Harvey.
It lived in a shiny cage with wire on top
and a front sliding wall of glass. There was
also a wheel that went around and around
when Harvey ran inside it. On the side of
the cage was a water bottle with a tube for
Harvey to drink from.

Before Tony left, he told Nicholas how to
take care of Harvey.

"You have to change the cedar shavings
in the cage every few days," he said. He
had brought a bag of them with him.

He had also brought a bag of special hamster food, which was made up of fourteen different kinds of seeds and nuts. "You can give him lettuce or carrot tops, too," Tony said. "But never, never give him any meat."

"Why not?" Nicholas asked.

Tony explained that, if hamsters were fed meat, they would get to like the taste of it so much they would try to eat each other when there was more than one hamster in a cage.

"That's called being 'carnivorous' or 'flesh eating,'" Tony said. "A hamster should stay 'herbivorous,' which is 'plant eating.'"

"Oh," said Nicholas. "Wow!" He would be very careful not to give Harvey any meat. "Can I take him out of his cage?" he asked as Tony was leaving.

"Sure," Tony said. "But watch out he doesn't disappear. So long." Then, halfway across the garden, he called, "Hey, I forgot to tell you. Hamsters are nocturnal, in case you didn't know. So long."

"What's that mean?" Nicholas called back. But Tony had already gone.

All that week Nicholas took good care of Harvey. He fed him and played with him and cleaned his cage carefully. But he always remembered that Harvey was Tony's hamster. He would hold it in his hand, feeling its little cold feet on his palm and its warm, quivering fur, and he would whisper, "Oh, I wish I had a hamster just like you!"

Harvey seemed to sleep most of the day, but at night he loved to run around and around inside his exercise wheel.

Nicholas loved the squeaky noise of Harvey's wheel. It put him to sleep at night just like a lullaby.

"Yes, I wish I had a hamster just like Harvey," Nicholas said sadly to himself.

All too soon the week was up. Tony would be coming home the next evening. After supper Nicholas decided to clean Harvey's cage for the last time.

He took it down to the kitchen. First he put Harvey in a large carton, where he could watch him. Then, very carefully, he slid out the glass panel from the cage, and very carefully he started to put the glass on the kitchen table, but all of a sudden . . . CRASH! The glass slipped from his hands and broke into a million pieces all over the kitchen floor!

Nicholas's father helped to sweep them up.

"We'll have to find some way of keeping Harvey in his cage until we can buy another piece of glass tomorrow morning," he said.

He found a piece of heavy cardboard, cut it to the right size, and slid it into the place where the glass had been. It worked very well.

When they had finished, it was time for Nicholas to go to bed. He was very sad because it was Harvey's last night in his house. He let Harvey play outside the cage for a longer time than usual. At last he put him in the cage and looked at him through the wires on top.

"Good night, Harvey," he whispered. "We sure had a good time, didn't we?" Then he turned out his light and soon fell asleep to the sound of the squeaking exercise wheel.

When morning came, Nicholas woke up
early to have as much time as possible with
Harvey before Tony came back. He looked
in through the top of the cage to say, "Good
morning," but . . . would you believe it? *The
cage was empty!*

"Oh, no!" Mother said when she heard.

"Ho ho," Father said when he went to
see. "He's chewed a hole right through the
cardboard. And I guess we are going to have
a grand time finding him!"

So they began to look — right then,
before breakfast. They looked under
Nicholas's bed. They looked in his dresser
drawers. They looked in his closet and in all
the boxes in the closet and in all the
pockets of all the clothes in the closet.

They looked in the toy soldier box and behind the curtains and under Nicholas's pillow and in between his blankets and inside his phonograph and even in his slippers.

When they had not found a trace of Harvey, Father sat down on Nicholas's bed.

"He could be anywhere, you know," he said gloomily. "Not just here in your room."

"And we'll never find him before Tony comes back," Nicholas said, and looked as though he might cry.

"What *are* we going to do?" Mother asked.

All at once, Father seemed to have the answer.

"We must go on a hunt for him," he said firmly. "As if he were a lion. Or an elephant. We must bring him back alive! And to do that, we must trap him." He jumped up. "First," he continued, "I'll need lots of plastic wastebaskets," and he looked at Mother.

"There's that little one in the bathroom," Mother said helpfully.

"No, no," Father said. "We must have lots more." And he dressed very quickly and rushed out of the house.

While he was gone, Nicholas and his mother continued to look for Harvey. They were still looking when Father came back with eight plastic wastebaskets. He also brought a new piece of glass for Harvey's cage.

"I borrowed the wastebaskets from the owner of the hardware store," he explained. "He was very interested in my plan."

"I can imagine," Mother said. "So am I. What is it?"

But Father was too busy to answer. He put a small pile of books in the middle of each room in the house and leaned a wastebasket against each pile so that the baskets were half lying, half standing.

"Now," he said, "I need blocks, long wooden blocks, Nicholas. And towels," he said to Mother. "Plenty of towels. And don't forget the lettuce."

"No," said Mother. "How could I forget the lettuce?"

So Father took the blocks and the towels and the lettuce and he made . . .

Hamster traps!

This is a hamster trap.

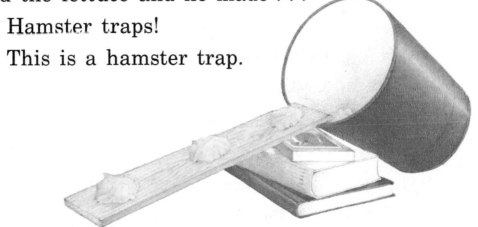

"Now, all we have to do is to wait for Harvey to eat his way up the ramp and fall into one of the wastebaskets," Father explained. "The plastic is too slippery for him to climb out." And he started to read his morning paper.

Mother looked at Nicholas.

"Do you think . . .?" Nicholas began.

"Not really," Mother said, and picked up her purse. "We'd better take a little shopping trip, just in case."

Mother took Nicholas to the pet store.

"We need a hamster, please," she said. "White, with pink eyes and a pink nose. About four inches long."

"I'm sorry," the pet store owner said. "We have only brown hamsters at the moment. Will they do?"

"No, no," Mother said. "They won't do at all. Thank you. We'll have to try somewhere else."

And they did. They tried many other places until quite late in the afternoon.

Mother telephoned Father from the next town where she and Nicholas had finally gone on their search.

"Father hasn't caught anything," she reported to Nicholas.

"And we haven't found another white hamster for Tony," Nicholas said, again feeling as if he might cry. "Now we'll have to buy him a brown one that won't even look like Harvey."

But when they got to the last pet shop, they were delighted to see a hamster that looked very much like Harvey. It was white with pink eyes and a pink nose, and it was just about four inches long, if you did not count its extra-long whiskers.

"That's the one," Mother said, and took out her purse. The shopkeeper put the hamster in a little cardboard box with air holes punched in top. Nicholas held it carefully on his lap on the way home. He felt much better now. At least Tony would have a hamster that could remind him of Harvey.

When they got home, Nicholas put the new hamster in Harvey's cage, which they'd taken to the kitchen. It ran around in Harvey's treadmill a few times. Then it curled up in a corner of the cage and went to sleep.

"I hope Tony will get to like you as much as he liked Harvey," Nicholas said to it. "Anyway, I like you. I wish you were my hamster."

"And I wish those traps had worked," Father said, looking at his wastebaskets. "I can't understand what went wrong." He picked up the now wilted lettuce leaves and threw them away. Nicholas put the blocks back in his room. Mother folded up the towels again.

"I don't know about you," she said, turning on the lamps in the living room, "but I'm exhausted. I am going to play myself some relaxing music." She sat down at the piano and turned the pages of her music book.

"A nocturne would do it," Father said, settling down to listen. Nicholas turned his head.

"A what?" he asked. Where had he heard that word before?

"A nocturne is a piece of night music, dreamy, cloudy kind of music. The word 'nocturne' has to do with night."

"Then that's what Tony meant," Nicholas cried, jumping up. "And that's why Harvey sleeps all day and plays all night. All hamsters do. They're nocturnal!"

He rushed into the dark kitchen, where, sure enough, the new hamster had awakened and was running furiously around Harvey's exercise wheel, just as Harvey used to do at night.

"Now is the time to look for Harvey," Nicholas shouted, running up the stairs to his room. He tiptoed over to his bed and sat down in the dark. Everything was very quiet. Then downstairs his mother started playing the nocturne — very softly. It sounded very nocturnal indeed. Nicholas listened, but he was also listening for something else — for the sound of a hamster waking up to play. What kind of sound would that be?

Then he heard it. A rustle and a scratch. And another rustle and another scratch! It came from underneath his bookshelf! Nicholas turned on his lamp, just in time to see Harvey's pink nose poking out from the tiniest crack between the bookshelf and the wall!

Nicholas waited until Harvey had squeezed himself out into the room, and then he swooped down and picked him up.

"I've got him!" he called to his parents, and ran downstairs.

"Good for you," Father said. "That's the way to hunt hamsters!"

"I never thought I'd consider a hamster so absolutely beautiful," said Mother, patting the top of Harvey's head with one finger. "How did you like my hamster music, Harvey?"

Then Nicholas put Harvey back in his cage. The two hamsters stared at each other for a moment. Then the new hamster returned to the exercise wheel and Harvey began to eat.

Nicholas and his parents watched them, and Nicholas began to feel a strange feeling of wildest hope. He looked at his mother and father. Did he dare to ask?

"Do you think . . ." he began, ". . . if I took very good care of him . . . that maybe . . .?" His mother and father nodded, almost together.

"Yes," his father said. "You're an expert on hamsters. I don't see why you shouldn't have one of your own."

"Yes," agreed Nicholas's mother. "I rather like hamsters now. We'll get him a cage in the morning. Tonight he can sleep in a plastic wastebasket."

Just then the doorbell rang. It was Tony. He had come to fetch Harvey.

He was very surprised to see another white hamster in Harvey's cage. Nicholas took his new hamster out, and it ran up his arm to sit on his shoulder.

"Hey," Tony said. "How come you got a hamster? It's not your birthday or anything, is it?"

Nicholas shook his head. "No," he said happily. "It was just by accident."

Tony was puzzled. "Oh," was all he said, as if he understood. But he didn't. He picked up Harvey's cage and the bags of food and shavings. "Well, thanks a lot for taking care of Harvey for me."

Nicholas went with him to the door. "You're welcome," he said. "See you tomorrow."

In the mirror next to the front door, Nicholas saw himself with his hamster. The hamster was sitting on Nicholas's head. It looked very happy up there, and underneath it Nicholas looked happy, too.

Hamsters

by Marci Ridlon

Hamsters are the nicest things
That anyone could own.
I like them even better than
Some dogs that I have known.

Their fur is soft, their faces nice.
They're small when they are grown.
And they sit inside your pocket
When you are all alone.

Night Animals

From the book

by Millicent E. Selsam

It is nighttime.

You are sleeping in your bed. Many of the animals outside are sleeping, too. But others are stirring. Let's see who is awake.

A little mouse steps softly out of its grassy nest. It is time to look for seeds, or berries, or nuts to nibble on.

But someone in the dark forest heard the tiny sounds the mouse made. Suddenly a shadow swoops down.

It is the screech owl. It closes its wings as it lands, ready to dig its hooked claws into the mouse.

But the mouse is gone. It ran back into its nest.

A big bullfrog is sitting in the pond. Its eyes seem to pop out of its head. If any small animal moves near, the frog's tongue will flash out. The animal will tumble into the frog's mouth.

A quiet movement among the trees makes you turn your head.

A deer is standing there. It lifts its thin legs high as it walks over to an oak tree and nibbles on the twigs.

The flying squirrel sitting in the moonlight looks like any other squirrel. But wait. It has a flap of skin connecting its front and back legs.

When it shoves off from the branch of a tree, it stretches out its legs, and glides 150 feet through the air.

The luna moth has just come out of her cocoon and spread her pale green wings. Soon she will give off a powerful odor into the night air.

Then a male luna moth will fly to her from more than five miles away. They will mate and the female luna will then fly around and deposit her eggs on the leaves of oak, willow, beech, and hickory trees.

The baby opossums are crawling all over their mother. Soon she will shove them off and find something for them to eat.

Maybe the wild cherries are ripe. Or perhaps the blackberries have turned juicy. If not, she can probably find a mouse or some worms.

Almost anything will do.

Five baby barn owls are sitting in the corner of an old barn. They are making clicking noises to show they are hungry.

The mother barn owl has to feed these baby birds for eight weeks. Then they, too, will leave the barn at night to find their own food.

The gray fox was hunting for food in the forest. Now he is taking a rest.

Meanwhile the red fox is hunting in the field at the edge of the forest.

Five black masks and five pairs of yellow eyes shine in the moonlight.

Five young racoons are out looking for food. They are on the way to a small pool where they will fish for crayfish and frogs.

Beavers are busy cutting down trees all through the night. This one is chewing on the bark of a young tree.

And this one has its teeth around a tree trunk. It will gnaw its way through until the tree falls.

The tiny lights of fireflies are twinkling on and off. Fireflies are not really flies. They are beetles. There are many different kinds of fireflies. Each kind of firefly has its own signal — its own special way of flashing its lights.

A female firefly sits at the tip of a blade of grass. A male firefly flies around her, flashing his lights. If it is the right signal, the female will flash back and the male will land beside her.

There are thousands of insects in the air above the lake. In one night a bat can eat hundreds of them.

This bat is skimming above the water, picking up insects. Every once in a while it will swoop down onto the lake and take a sip of water.

There are baby rabbits in this nest. A quick movement — what was that?

As mother rabbit turns to look, a weasel slips by.

The baby rabbits are safe for a while.

The porcupine is sitting in a pine tree. Its quills look like a bundle of pine needles.

The sweet smell of raspberries reaches its nose. Now the porcupine will back down the trunk and waddle over to the bushes where the berries are ripe. There it will feast until its belly is full.

A mother skunk and her three babies are taking a walk in the forest. As she goes along, the mother skunk turns up stones and digs into rotten stumps. Maybe juicy caterpillars and worms are hiding there.

She may also catch a mouse or a cricket on the forest floor. There she will share the food with her young ones.

A pale light appears in the sky.

Night is over.

The foxes will go back to their dens.

The beavers will go back to their lodges.

The racoons will go back to their holes in a tree.

The bats will go back to their caves or hollow trees and hang upside down.

The porcupine will climb up a tall tree and stretch out between two big branches.

All the other animals of the night will find a place to rest during the day.

Then the sun will come up. The day animals will start to wake up.

You, too.

THE TALE OF
PETER RABBIT

WRITTEN AND ILLUSTRATED BY
BEATRIX POTTER

Once upon a time there were four little Rabbits, and their names were — Flopsy, Mopsy, Cotton-tail, and Peter.

They lived with their Mother in a sand-bank, underneath the root of a very big fir-tree.

"Now, my dears," said old Mrs. Rabbit one morning, "you may go into the fields or down the lane, but don't go into Mr. McGregor's garden. Your Father had an accident there. He was put in a pie by Mrs. McGregor."

"Now run along, and don't get into mischief. I am going out."

Then old Mrs. Rabbit took a basket and her umbrella, and went through the wood to the baker's. She bought a loaf of brown bread and five currant buns.

Flopsy, Mopsy, and Cottontail, who were good little bunnies, went down the lane to gather blackberries.
But Peter, who was very naughty, ran straight away to Mr. McGregor's garden, and squeezed under the gate!

First he ate some lettuces and some French beans, and then he ate some radishes. And then, feeling rather sick, he went to look for some parsley.

But round the end of a cucumber frame, whom should he meet but Mr. McGregor!

Mr. McGregor was on
his hands and knees
planting out young
cabbages, but he
jumped up and ran
after Peter, waving a
rake and calling out,
"Stop thief!"

Peter was most dreadfully frightened. He
rushed all over the garden, for he had
forgotten the way back to the gate.

He lost one of his shoes among the
cabbages, and the other shoe amongst the
potatoes.

After losing them, he ran on four legs and went faster, so that I think he might have got away altogether if he had not unfortunately run into a gooseberry net, and got caught by the large buttons on his jacket. It was a blue jacket with brass buttons, quite new.

Peter gave himself up for lost, and shed big tears, but his sobs were overheard by some friendly sparrows, who flew to him in great excitement, and implored him to exert himself.

Mr. McGregor came up with a sieve, which he intended to pop upon the top of Peter, but Peter wriggled out just in time, leaving his jacket behind him.

And rushed into the toolshed, and jumped into a can. It would have been a beautiful thing to hide in, if it had not had so much water in it.

Mr. McGregor was quite sure that Peter was somewhere in the tool-shed, perhaps hidden underneath a flower-pot. He began to turn them over carefully, looking under each.

Presently Peter sneezed — "Kertyschoo!" Mr. McGregor was after him in no time.

And tried to put his foot upon Peter, who jumped out of a window, upsetting three plants. The window was too small for Mr. McGregor, and he was tired of running after Peter. He went back to his work.

Peter sat down to rest. He was out of breath and trembling with fright, and he had not the least idea which way to go. Also he was very damp with sitting in that can.

After a time he began to wander about, going lippity — lippity — not very fast, and looking all round.

He found a door in a wall, but it was locked, and there was no room for a fat little rabbit to squeeze underneath.

An old mouse was running in and out over the stone doorstep, carrying peas and beans to her family in the wood. Peter asked her the way to the gate, but she had such a large pea in her mouth that she could not answer. She only shook her head at him. Peter began to cry.

Then he tried to find his way straight across the garden, but he became more and more puzzled. Presently, he came to a pond where Mr. McGregor filled his water-cans. A white cat was staring at some gold-fish. She sat very, very still, but now and then the tip of her tail twitched as if it were alive. Peter thought it best to go away without speaking to her. He had heard about cats from his cousin, little Benjamin Bunny.

He went back towards the tool-shed, but suddenly, quite close to him, he heard the noise of a hoe — scr-r-ritch, scratch, scratch, scritch. Peter scuttered underneath the bushes. But presently, as nothing happened, he came out, and climbed upon a wheelbarrow and peeped over. The first thing he saw was Mr. McGregor hoeing onions. His back was turned towards Peter, and beyond him was the gate!

Peter got down very quietly off the wheelbarrow, and started running as fast as he could go, along a straight walk behind some black-currant bushes.

Mr. McGregor caught sight of him at the corner, but Peter did not care. He slipped

underneath the gate, and was safe at last in the wood outside the garden.

Mr. McGregor hung up the little jacket and the shoes for a scare-crow to frighten the blackbirds.

Peter never stopped running or looked behind him till he got home to the big fir-tree.

He was so tired that he flopped down upon the nice soft sand on the floor of the rabbit-hole and shut his eyes. His mother was busy cooking. She wondered what he had done with his clothes. It was the second little jacket and pair of shoes that Peter had lost in a fortnight!

I am sorry to say that Peter was not very well during the evening.

His mother put him to bed, and made some camomile tea, and she gave a dose of it to Peter!

"One table-spoonful to be taken at bed-time."

But Flopsy, Mopsy, and Cotton-tail had bread and milk and blackberries for supper.

THE END

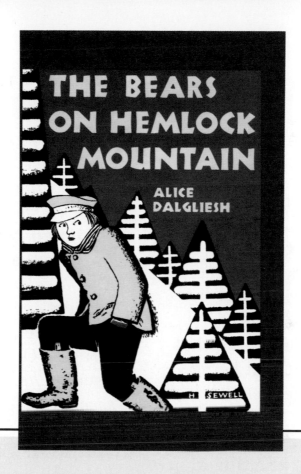

You have read about some "great escapes." Now read about Jonathan.

Will he escape from danger when he is all alone on Hemlock Mountain? You'll find out when you read *The Bears on Hemlock Mountain* by Alice Dalgliesh.

Glossary

A

above   At a higher level: *My room is above hers.*

absolutely   Certainly; without a doubt: *I am absolutely sure that one plus one is two.*

accident   Something that happens without being planned: *We met by accident.*

adventure   A dangerous, unusual, or exciting experience: *Hiking up there is an adventure!*

ambulance   A car that takes people to a hospital quickly.

angry   Feeling that you are not pleased with someone or something: *Jed was so angry that he slammed the door.*

announce   To make something known: *Jay announced the winner.*

assure   To give someone confidence: *The doctor assured the girl that her broken arm would heal.*

astonished   Greatly surprised; amazed: *Everyone was astonished when it snowed in April.*

automobile   A car.

average   Ordinary or usual: *The average seven-year-old loves pizza.*

awfully   **1.** Very: *The baby is awfully tired.* **2.** Very badly: *Our team performed awfully this year.*

B

badger   A small animal with short legs that lives underground.

barely Almost not at all; just a little bit: *We had barely enough to eat.*

believe To think something is true or real: *Do you believe in the Tooth Fairy?*

bellow To make a loud roar: *When the bull was angry, he bellowed.*

bitterly Sharply unpleasant: *On bitterly cold days we stay inside.*

bliss Very great happiness: *The music was so lovely we were in bliss.*

borrow To get something from someone else with the understanding that it will be returned or replaced: *May I please borrow your pencil?*

boulder A large, rounded rock.

bramble A plant that has thorny stems and fruit that can be eaten: *Blackberries are brambles.*

bray A donkey's loud cry: *The donkey brayed when we put the load on it.*

burro A small donkey.

business 1. A person's work or activity: *He's in the business of selling houses.* 2. Something of concern or interest: *This problem is none of your business.*

C

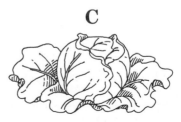

cabbage A plant with a rounded head and tight, overlapping leaves that is eaten as a vegetable.

cabin   A small wooden house: *On our vacation, we stayed at a cabin in the mountains.*

camomile   A plant that is used to make tea: *After dinner, we'll have camomile tea.*

candle   A stick of wax with a string going through the middle that is burned to make light: *When the electricity was off, we had to light candles.*

canter   Gallop slowly and easily: *At our next riding lesson we will learn to canter.*

canyon   A deep valley with steep walls on all sides.

carve   To make by cutting: *William likes to carve animals out of wood.*

certainly   Definitely; without a doubt: *I will certainly come to your party.*

clever   Smart; able to think quickly.

cobbler   A person who makes or fixes shoes.

cocoon   The silky covering spun by a caterpillar to protect itself until it turns into a moth or butterfly: *If you look carefully, you will see the cocoon hanging from a leaf.*

coin   A piece of metal made by the government to be used as money: *Coins are often used to pay for things.*

comfortable   Giving comfort: *These clothes are comfortable because they fit well.*

condition   **1.** Something that is required before some other thing can happen: *You may play on the condition that you do your homework first.* **2.** The way someone or something is: *Her bicycle is in poor condition.*

connect To link or join: *On this page, draw a line connecting the two boxes.*

consider To think over before deciding: *I will consider trading toys with you.*

continue Keep on: *The car broke down, so we continued by train.*

country The land away from cities and large towns: *My uncle has a large farm in the country.*

crayfish A freshwater animal that looks like a lobster but is much smaller.

cucumber A long vegetable with green skin and white, watery flesh: *Put cucumbers and carrots in the salad.*

cucumber frame A wooden structure that helps a farmer to grow cucumbers: *The vines have begun to climb the cucumber frame.*

D

danger A harmful situation: *If you go near the edge, you'll be in danger of falling.*

dangerous Full of danger; able to damage or cause harm: *That knife is dangerous.*

deaf Unable to hear: *Because the girl was deaf, she learned to use sign language.*

decide To make up one's mind: *Ann decided to have vanilla instead of chocolate ice cream.*

decorate To dress up with something beautiful or attractive: *We decorated the room with balloons and posters.*

decoration Something that decorates, adorns, or dresses up: *The party decorations looked wonderful.*

deer Animals that chew the cud and have hooves. The males have antlers: *Many deer live in the woods near my house.*

delicious Tasting very good: *The pie was so delicious I ate two pieces.*

den The shelter or home of a wild animal: *Foxes and lions live in dens.*

deposit **1.** To lay or to put down: *I'll deposit my books on the desk.* **2.** To put money in the bank: *Dad deposited his check.*

develop To come slowly into being: *You can develop good habits.*

difficult Hard to understand: *That is a difficult math problem.*

disappear To go out of sight: *At noon the fog disappeared.*

discover To find out; to learn: *I looked down and discovered my shoelace was untied.*

doe A female deer. (See *deer.*)

dose An amount of medicine to be taken at one time: *The doctor said to take a small dose.*

dreadfully Awfully; terribly: *That dog looks dreadfully sick.*

E

early Happening near the beginning of something: *We ate an early breakfast.*

earn To get money by working: *How much do you earn for delivering papers?*

echo A sound that gets repeated when sound waves bounce off a surface: *When you shout in the basement, you can hear an echo.*

edge   The line where an object or area ends: *Ana sat down on the edge of the bed.*

effect   A result; something that happens because of something else: *The opened shades have a nice effect on the room.*

elves   Make-believe creatures who have magical powers and can be helpful or mischievous: *The little elves in my storybook have big ears.*

exactly   **1.** In every way: *The twins looked exactly alike.* **2.** Without any mistake: *There are exactly fifty-cards in this box.*

excited   Stirred up: *We were very excited about the party.*

excuse   To free from having to do something: *Father will excuse you from dinner.*

exercise   Physical activity or movement for the good of the body: *Get some exercise every day.*

exert   To put into use: *You must exert energy when jumping rope.*

exhausted   To be completely worn out; to be very tired: *I am exhausted from that long walk.*

expert   A person who has knowledge or skill in a special area: *My mother is an expert in plant care.*

F

farther   To or at a greater distance: *The farther we walked into the woods, the more lost we became.*

female   A person or animal that is of the sex that can be a mother to young ones: *The owner of the pet store said the turtle was female.*

fetch To go after and get: *Jill went to fetch some water.*

fiddlesticks An expression of mild annoyance or impatience: *Oh fiddlesticks! I lost my pen.*

flash **1.** A very short time: *We ate lunch in a flash.* **2.** A sudden burst of light: *There was a quick flash of lightning.*

fortnight A period of two weeks: *We can expect another letter in a fortnight.*

fray To become so worn away that loose threads show: *The old tablecloth was frayed and torn.*

frightened Became afraid: *I was so frightened by the loud noise, I couldn't move.*

furiously With great anger or violence: *The waves crashed furiously against the rocks.*

future The time that is to come: *I had a dream about what might happen in the future.*

G

general **1.** Not limited or specialized: *It seems like that general store sells everything!* **2.** Related to or involving all: *There was general excitement in the crowd.*

gentleness The condition of being kind and thoughtful: *Aunt Rosa is loved by all for her gentleness.*

giant A very large person in a make-believe story: *My little sister loves to read stories about giants.*

glisten To shine in the light: *The snow glistened in the sunlight.*

gnaw To chew or bite on: *Some animals gnaw on dead trees.*

gobble To eat quickly or in a greedy manner: *I was so hungry I gobbled up my lunch.*

graze To feed on growing grass: *Cows like to graze on hillsides.*

greetings An expression of welcome; a way to say hello: *Greetings, friends!*

grocery A store that sells food and things for the house. *This bag is full of things from the grocery store.*

group Persons or things gathered together: *Groups of children are playing in the park.*

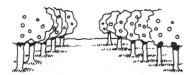

grove A group of trees with open ground between them: *Let's visit the orange groves.*

guardian Someone who guards, defends, or protects: *That man acts as guardian of the castle.*

gurgle To make a bubbling sound: *The baby gurgled as he drank from his bottle.*

H

hamper A large covered basket used for holding laundry: *We were asked to put our dirty clothes in the hamper.*

hamster A small animal with soft fur, large cheek pouches, and a short tail: *A hamster can make a good pet.*

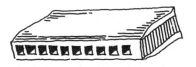

harmonica A small musical instrument that is played by blowing in and out through a set of holes.

haughty Proud of oneself while looking down on others: *In Snow White, the queen was the haughtiest woman in the land.*

herd A group of animals that stay together: *A herd of cattle was standing inside the fence.*

hero A person who is admired for being brave or for doing something special: *Sam was a hero for having brought home the lost dog.*

hogan An earth-covered Indian house: *The family slept inside the hogan.*

hollow 1. A small valley: *There are pine trees in the hollow.* 2. Having space or an opening inside: *The body of a guitar is hollow.*

horrible Very unpleasant: *This soup tastes horrible.*

hospital A place where sick or hurt people go to get better: *Three people were taken to the hospital because of the accident.*

I

imagine To make a picture in one's mind; to get an idea of: *Imagine how silly we looked!*

implore To ask; to beg: *We implored them to help us.*

intend To have a plan in mind: *We intended to go to the zoo.*

K

kangaroo An animal that has short front legs and powerful back legs for jumping: *The mother kangaroo carried her baby in her pouch.*

kindness   The condition of being helpful, gentle, or generous: *We thanked the man for his kindness.*

L

ladies'   Something belonging to, or for the use of, two or more women: *The ladies' hat shop is on this street.*

layer   A single thickness of material covering a surface: *The leaves had a thin layer of ice on them.*

listen   To pay attention: *Please listen to my story.*

locomotive   An engine used to pull or push railroad cars along a track: *The locomotive made a lot of noise as it entered the station.*

lodge   The shelter or home of certain animals, such as the rounded home built by beavers: *At night, the beaver swims to his lodge to sleep.*

lodged   To become stuck or caught: *The lion had a splinter lodged in his paw.*

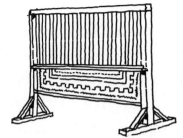

loom   A machine or frame used for weaving cloth: *I will use this loom to weave a large rug for the bedroom.*

lumber   1. To move clumsily or heavily: *The bears lumbered through the forest.* 2. Wooden boards made from trees: *They will use the lumber to build a new porch.*

M

magic   The pretended art of making things happen using charms or spells: *The woman disappeared suddenly, as if by magic.*

male A person or animal of the sex that is a father to young ones: *A male chicken is called a rooster.*

manage 1. To succeed in doing something: *I did manage to work hard and have fun at the same time.* 2. To have control over: *Who will manage the store while I am gone?*

market A place where things are bought and sold: *We'll buy vegetables at the market.*

medium-sized A size between small and large: *Taki ate a medium-sized apple for lunch.*

mesa A hill with a flat top and tall sides: *From the top of the mesa you can see quite far.*

misbehavior Bad behavior: *Sue was sorry for her misbehavior.*

mischief Naughty behavior: *What kind of mischief are you up to?*

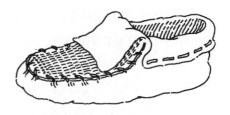

moccasin A soft leather shoe that has no heel: *Father wears moccasins lined with fur in the winter.*

moment Minute; instant: *Both the phone and the doorbell rang at the same moment.*

moose A large, heavy animal with big, broad antlers.

mountain An area of land that rises very high: *The mountains are covered with snow at this time of year.*

music   Sounds that go together in a pleasing or meaningful way: *John says that listening to music makes him happy.*

N

neighbor   A person who lives next door to or near another: *Our family shares a backyard with two other neighbors.*

nephew   The son of one's brother or sister: *Aunt Tina let her nephew Tim drive her new car.*

nibble   To eat with small, quick bites: *Mice nibble their food.*

nocturne   Music that reminds us of nighttime: *When my father played the nocturne, I felt sleepy.*

North Pole   The most northern point of the earth: *Aside from scientists and explorers, few people have been to the North Pole.*

nudge   To push in a gentle way: *The mother bird nudged her baby out of the nest.*

O

occasion   A very important event: *My birthday is a special occasion for me.*

occasionally   Happening from time to time: *I occasionally read in the sun but I prefer to read in the shade.*

odor   Smell; scent: *The odor of frying bacon made my mouth water.*

opossum   A furry animal that lives mostly in trees and carries its young in a pouch: *Maybe you'll see an opossum when you go camping.*

P

pardon To excuse: *Pardon me for stepping on your foot.*

phooey An exclamation of dislike or disgust: *Phooey! I don't like peas.*

piñon A pine tree found in western United States: *We played under the piñon tree.*

pity A reason for regret or sadness: *It's a pity that he's sick.*

poem A piece of writing, often in rhyme, in which words are chosen for their sound and beauty as well as meaning: *This is my favorite poem.*

politely With good manners and courtesy.

poor **1.** Deserving pity, unfortunate: *That poor puppy is cold.* **2.** Having little or no money; owning few things: *They are too poor to buy new chairs.*

porcupine An animal whose back and sides are covered with long, sharp quills.

possum Another name for an opossum. (See *opossum.*)

potato A vegetable that has firm white flesh and grows underground: *My sister made soup with carrots and potatoes in it.*

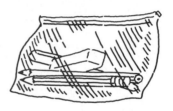

pouch A bag of soft material, such as leather or cloth, for carrying various things: *I always carry my pencils in this plastic pouch.*

precious Having great value: *Gold is a precious metal.*

presently In a short time; soon: *I'll catch up with you presently.*

private For a particular person or group; not public: *Carol needed a* private *place to practice her part for the play.*

promise A statement that someone will do something: *If I* promise *to do my homework first, may I go skating with you and Dad?*

Q

question Something that is asked: *I want to ask you a* question.

quietness The condition of being silent, nearly silent, or calm: *The library is the best place to read because of the* quietness *there.*

quill **1.** The sharp, hollow spine of a porcupine: *Porcupines use their* quills *against enemies.* **2.** A long feather: *Long ago, people wrote with* quill *pens.*

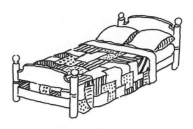

quilt A bed cover: *This* quilt *will help keep you warm.*

quite Completely: *Henry has not* quite *finished eating his breakfast.*

quiver To shake lightly or tremble: *My hand was* quivering *as I touched the snake.*

R

radish A red or white vegetable: *Radishes taste best right from the garden.*

responsibility Something that a person is depended on for doing: *Drying the dishes is your* responsibility.

revolting Awful; disgusting: *The garbage had a* revolting *smell.*

reward Something given in exchange for an important service: *You were so brave that you should get a reward.*

rust **1.** A reddish-brown coating that forms on metal: *The metal pail will rust if you leave it out in the rain.* **2.** A reddish-brown color: *Angela wore a black sweater with rust pants.*

rustle A soft, fluttering sound: *The rustle of leaves was all around us in the woods.*

S

scissors A tool that cuts: *Use these scissors to cut out the picture.*

scowl A lowering of the eyebrows in anger; a frown: *Why are you scowling at me?*

scurry To move lightly and quickly: *Mice scurried across the floor.*

sedge grass A plant that looks like grass, but has a solid rather than a hollow stem: *When is the best time to plant sedge grass?*

seldom Not often; rarely: *Since we moved, we seldom see our old friends.*

sensible Reasonable, showing good judgment: *Be sensible and wear boots in the rain.*

shyness The condition of being bashful or timid: *Both cousins are known for their shyness.*

sieve A container that has tiny holes in the bottom to let only water or small pieces of material pass through: *Maybe we will find shells if we pour sand through the sieve.*

sight 1. A view: *I caught sight of the bird as it flew from the tree.* 2. The ability to see: *Grandfather's sight is very good.*

signal A sign that gives information; a warning: *The signal to stop is a red light.*

simply Merely, just: *I was simply sitting there.*

sob To cry loudly: *The child was sobbing because he was lost and afraid.*

softness The condition of being smooth or pleasing to feel or look at: *We chose the white blanket because of its softness.*

South Pole The most southern point of the earth: *Do any animals live near the South Pole?*

special Different from what is common or usual: *Because it was a special occasion, we took a bouquet of flowers.*

sprang back Returned to its original position: *Nina pushed aside the tree branch, but it sprang back.*

spring The time of year between winter and summer: *My favorite flowers are the ones that bloom in the spring.*

squat To sit on your heels: *We were squatting down to paint the bottom of the fence.*

squirm Twist around; wiggle: *Mike's teacher told him to stop squirming, and sit still.*

squirrel A furry animal with a bushy tail: *The squirrel is busy gathering nuts.*

startle To fill with sudden fear: *The dog was startled at the sound of the car's horn.*

steer To guide the direction of: *Learning to steer a bicycle is difficult at first.*

stroller A light carriage that carries small children: *This is a perfect day to take the baby for a walk in the stroller.*

surrounded Having something on all sides: *The mouse, surrounded by cats, ran back into its hole.*

swell Fine, excellent: *We had a swell time at the beach.*

T

tantrum An outburst of bad temper: *Liz cried and screamed when she threw a tantrum.*

terrific Very great, extreme: *The thunder made a terrific "boom!"*

thief A person who steals things or money: *Catch that thief before he escapes with my wallet!*

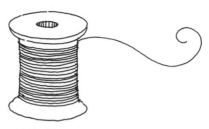

thread 1. A fine, thin cord used for sewing or weaving: *He bought enough thread to sew three more buttons onto his jacket.* 2. To pass one end of a thread or string through a hole: *Max threaded the needle carefully.*

tide The regular rising and falling of the level of the oceans: *It is best to go fishing at high tide.*

tide pool A pool of water remaining on the beach after the tide goes out: *See how many crabs you can count in the tide pool.*

ton 2,000 pounds: *That elephant must weigh at least a ton.*

tornado A storm with strong winds in the shape of a funnel or cone: *Several houses on our side of town were damaged by the tornado.*

tortoise A turtle that lives on land: *In the summer, we found a tortoise near the baseball field.*

toward In the direction of: *We walked toward the pond.*

tremble To shake from fear or cold: *The day was so cold that we trembled.*

trouble A difficult, dangerous, or upsetting situation: *We'll be in trouble if we don't get home before dark.*

turkey A large bird that is raised for food: *Carmen invited me over for a turkey dinner.*

U

unfortunately Without luck: *Unfortunately, the rain did not stop all day.*

V

valley An area of low land between mountains or hills: *The grass is always green in the valley.*

vegetable A plant whose roots, leaves, stems, or flowers can be eaten: *We grow vegetables in the garden.*

village A small town: *Tonight there is going to be a party in the village where I live.*

violin A musical instrument that has four strings and is played with a bow: *I practice one hour a day on the violin.*

W

waddle To take short steps and move from side to side: *Look at the duck waddle toward the pond!*

wander To move from place to place without a special purpose: *We wandered all around that strange and wonderful city.*

wares Things for sale: *At the market, the craftsman showed his wares.*

warn To tell of coming danger: *The radio warned the town of the coming storm.*

wedge To crowd or squeeze into a small space: *See if you can wedge that rock between those two pieces of wood.*

whale A large sea animal that, unlike fish, needs air to breathe and gives milk to its babies.

whole Entire: *The whole class is going on a trip.*

wintry Of or relating to winter or cold: *The wintry day reminded us that winter would soon be here.*

wonderful Very good; excellent: *I saw a wonderful movie.*

weasel An animal with soft fur and a long, narrow body that eats small animals and birds.

world The earth: *Sometimes airplanes fly all over the world.*

Continued from page 2.

Credits

Cover Design: James Stockton & Associates

Illustrators: 8–9 Maxie Chambliss
10–18 Arnold Lobel **19** Lynne Cherry
20–40 James Marshall **41** Ron Barrett
42–43 Lynne Cherry **44–55** Eric Jon Nones
56 Carol Schwartz **57–65** Mai Vo-Dinh
66–74 Meg Kelleher Aubrey **75** Peter E.
Hanson **78–89** Derek Steele **90** Carol
Inouye **91–105** Nancy Edwards Calder
106–126 Evaline Ness **127** Bill Peet
128–129 Jim Henterly **130–143** Jose Aruego
and Ariane Dewey **144–161** H. A. Rey
162 Susan Considine **163** Bernard Waber
164–165 Philip Argent **166–176** Pat and
Robin DeWitt **177** Stella Ormai
178–188 Philippe Fix **189** Paul O. Zelinsky
192–212 Ronald Himler **213–227** Margaret
Sanfilippo **228–229** Anna Vojtech
230–244 Alan Baker **245** Vera B. Williams
248–254 Carol Leeson **255** Susan Russo
256–266 Karen Gundersheimer **267** Nonny
Hogrogian **268–269** Jim Henterly
270–290 Diet Van Beek **291** Alan Baker
304–318 Beatrix Potter **319** Helen Sewell

Photographers: 76–77 Andrew Parsons Photography **190–191** J.C. Carton/Bruce Coleman
246–247 David Perry **292** Leonard Lee Rue
III/National Audubon/Photo Researchers
293 (top) Eric Hosking/Photo Researchers,
(bottom) Leonard Lee Rue III/Animals, Animals
294 (top) Jerome Wexler/Photo Researchers,
(bottom) Leonard Lee Rue III/DPI **295** (top)
Ed Cesar/National Audubon/Photo Researchers,
(bottom) Ed Rescher/Peter Arnold **296** New York
Zoological Society **297** (top & bottom) Karl H.
Maslowski/Photo Researchers **298** Leonard Lee
Rue III/Animals, Animals **299** (top & bottom)
Rota/American Museum of Natural History
300 Leonard Lee Rue III/Photo Researchers
301 (top) F. Overton/American Museum of
Natural History, (bottom) Leonard Lee Rue
III/Animals, Animals **302** H. Charles
Laun/Photo Researchers